MW01166195

Notes in the Key of C

Tuning out Cancer, Tuning in Hope

John David Morgan

Notes in the Key of C

Tuning out Cancer, Tuning in Hope

©2023, John David Morgan

All rights reserved. This book or any portion thereof may not be reproduced or used in any manner whatsoever without the express written permission of the publisher except for the use of brief quotations in a book review.

Cover photo -Tim Johnson

ISBN: 979-8-35092-039-0

ISBN eBook: 979-8-35092-040-6

Dedication

"Dedicated to the One I Love"

– THE MAMAS AND THE PAPAS

The stories in this book focus primarily on cancer patients, but the unsung heroes here are the nurses, techs, and admins. I admire their tenacity, and I'm continually amazed by their tireless, smiling faces as they care for their patients.

Over the years, I've roamed the halls of many hospital departments with guitar in hand. In each place, the staff has consistently modeled empathy and compassion. I've witnessed care that goes beyond meeting medical needs and reaches deep to relieve the patient's fears and concerns. The staff knows this journey is difficult and human connection is an essential element of the healing process.

At times, there is a high demand for immediate attention in the midst of an already fast-paced environment. One day, I heard a female voice echoing down the hall. "Doctor! Nurse! Doctor! Nurse! Help me, help me! Somebody help me!"

A nurse walked into the room and things got quiet. Seconds after the nurse left, the mournful pleading began again. From a distance, I saw this cycle play out several times.

The patient was being well cared for and not in any pain. I asked the nurse if some music might help. "You can give it a try," she said with a smile and a slight eye roll.

When I stepped into the room, I saw a middle-aged woman with wild gray hair flaring out in every direction. Her makeup looked like she was ready for an evening on the town but had neglected to use a mirror to apply it.

"Would you like to hear some music?"

She stared at me blankly for half a minute then said, "No."

When I stepped back into the hallway, she continued her well-worn refrain. I saw the nurse a few minutes later and asked if that had been going on all day.

"All day," she replied. "But it's not her, it's the disease. The cancer is affecting her brain. If she were in her right mind and could see herself acting like this, she would be completely embarrassed. Her daughter will be here later this afternoon and things will calm down."

The nurse's level of care, showing so much respect and kindness for this difficult patient, demonstrated what it means to recognize the value of every person. I've had the privilege of seeing this level of compassion in action regularly for the past twenty years.

These stories are dedicated to the caring women and men who have chosen the healing road. This song is for you.

Contents

Prelude

"Waiting For My Real Life to Begin"

– COLIN HAY

It seems we artistic types spend a lot of time waiting for that life-changing phone call, email, or text. The connection that will launch us to the next level, the next step into what we were always meant to be. We're always scanning the horizon for our proverbial ship to come in.

When my ship came in, it looked more like a rowboat. I received a phone call from a friend asking if I could play music for hospitalized cancer patients. The exact question was, "Can you play instrumental music at 10:00 am on Tuesday once every two months?" Little did I know how that beautiful little rowboat would be my transportation through life for the next twenty years. The current carried me from room to room and into many beautiful lives.

Why this book? It's a celebration of humanity, of people and their stories. Beyond that, it's for anyone whose life has been touched by cancer or has walked the journey alongside a friend or family member.

These accounts are told from memory. I have tried to represent every story and situation as honestly and as accurately as possible. Of course, out of respect for the privacy of the people I've worked with and in accordance with HIPAA (Health Insurance Portability and Accountability Act) regulations, the names of all patients and hospital staff have been changed. I am fortunate to have a very HIPAA-compliant mind when it comes to remembering names!

For years, the thought of writing a book never occurred to me. When I got together with friends, the inevitable "what's new?" question would come up. I would say, "Well, today at the hospital..." Their next question was, "Are you writing this stuff down?" The answer at that time was "no," but the message got through. I started scratching down a few details and those chicken scratches turned into stories. When those fragmented notes overflowed a three-ring binder, the "You've got to write a book" became inevitable.

Most chapter titles and section headings are song titles. The song may not be directly related to the story, but then again, it may. Songs and their titles are like that. If nothing else, these songs would make an outstanding playlist.

Where we're from is part of who we are, so you will also find a few stories of my growing up in the small river town of Gallipolis, Ohio. A quirky guy from a quirky town.

Full disclosure: I'm a guitar nut. I enjoy guitar music of all kinds, so expect to find a little guitar geekiness sprinkled throughout.

My secret purpose in writing this book is to plant seeds in other musicians who feel a calling to healing work. If reading these stories makes you think, *I could do that!* then please do. Grab the oars. This may be your rowboat.

1

"Beginnings"

— CHICAGO

"Telephone Line"

– ELECTRIC LIGHT ORCHESTRA

In 2001, the first wave of the ".com" era was imploding, crashing under the weight of its overly optimistic expectations. Everyone knew the internet was the next big thing and was looking to stake a claim in the digital frontier. Unfortunately, no one was sure where or how to start digging to find the gold. Like many others, the dot-com business I was managing turned into a dot-bomb, and it was time for me to start looking for another corporate position.

Soon after I'd started that search, terrorists crashed planes into the World Trade Center. The job prospects I was pursuing dried up. It was tough enough being a middle-aged middle manager, and the tragedy of 911 locked up the hiring process for many businesses. How could anyone plan for the future when the whole world had just turned upside down?

I knew I couldn't sit around and wait for a job to find me. Then a crazy idea popped into my head. *I've been playing and teaching guitar since college, one or two students at a time plus occasional group lessons. Maybe this could be turned into a business.* My wife, Connie, and I discussed it. She had a good job, the kids were grown and doing well. Let's give it a try for a year.

For starters, I began to write down everything I wish I had known when I first started playing the guitar. I checked out several book/music stores to see what other instructors were teaching.

Though I was familiar with most of the available instructional material, there is always something new coming out. I didn't find anything along the lines of the approach I had in mind. I went home, closed the curtains, quit answering the phone, and began to write.

Aside from a handful of regular students and coffeehouse/bookstore gigging, the only thing I did during this time was write and rewrite. In the back of my mind was a lingering question: Is music a frivolous human pursuit, or is it something substantial enough to build into a career? Looming large was the stereotype of the guy who thinks he's the next James Taylor/Eric Clapton/Neil Young/Bob Dylan but who never makes it beyond the local circuit.

Six weeks later, I emerged from my self-imposed isolation with *Foundations for Great Guitar Playing* completed. It was my very own spiral-bound book with two audio CDs included.

Around this same time, I received a call from *Business First,* the local business newspaper. They were working on an article called "Sitting it Out," telling the stories of professionals from tech industries who had lost jobs thanks to the bursting of the .com bubble. My guitar and I got a decent-size picture on the front page of the Local section. Nice, but I would have preferred being on "The Cover of 'Rolling Stone.'"

One day while writing, studying, practicing, and teaching, I received a phone call from a friend. Becky told me she was helping to put together a roster of musicians who would be willing to play music at a hospital in downtown Columbus. Each person would play in the hallways of the cancer floor from 10:00 to 11:00 AM on Tuesday mornings. With eight musicians in the rotation, each of us would only need to do this once every two months.

"That sounds like a good thing. Let me check my calendar." (As if I needed to look. My morning hours were as empty as a frozen farm field in winter.) "Yes, I'm available, but only until I get back into the corporate world, which may be very soon."

I played once every other month at the hospital for two years. Then one day, one of the housekeeping ladies said, "It sure is good to hear you."

"Thanks, but you have live music every Tuesday, don't you?"

"Nope, you're the only one still coming."

A week later, I was walking across a street—actually, it was a small alley dwarfed by tall medical buildings on either side—when an attractive young woman loaded with art supplies stopped me in the middle of the alley and said, "I'm the art therapist. I know who you are, and I know what you're doing. When I get a budget, I want to hire you for the big hospital."

This was completely out of the blue. I didn't think anybody knew where I was or what I was doing. My first thought was *Uhhh, my name is John. I play guitar*. What came out of my mouth was, "Uhhh, sounds great. Here's my business card."

Approximately a year and a half later, I was praying, "Lord, I need to figure out how to make this music thing work." The number of students had continued to grow. Sales of CDs were a slow but steady trickle. My book was being used as the main curriculum for worship leader training at Vineyard Church of Columbus. All of this was good, but not quite a career. And there had been no word from the art therapist. I found out her name was Jennifer. Another great idea lost at sea.

Suddenly, a mental flash: Gigging, more gigging, larger venues, bigger crowds. That's the way to do this. "Lord, please open this door.

I don't care how large the audience is. Please let me get in front of the teeming masses so I can make a decent living."

Four days later, I received the call. "Hi, John, this is Jennifer, the art therapist. We met a while ago. I've got the budget. Meet me in the hospital cafeteria next Tuesday, and I'll explain what you need to do. By the way, you'll be playing for patients, one or two, maybe three people at a time. I hope that's all right."

"That's fine. I don't care how large the audience is."

Since that time, the masses have been less than teeming, but I have played for thousands of people—one, two, maybe three at a time.

When I got the call, I was simply a musician looking for a gig. There's always the possibility that a famous record executive, home from California to visit his ailing mother, will walk through the hospital, hear me, and immediately sign me to a super-duper record contract. There is also an equal possibility that one day pigs will sprout wings and fly. Neither has happened yet.

What I didn't realize when I walked into this opportunity was that I had unwittingly stepped into a completely new universe, a place that would prove more rewarding than any record deal. Not to be overly dramatic, but I would soon discover that this was the calling I had been preparing for all my life.

"I Won't Back Down"

– TOM PETTY AND THE HEARTBREAKERS

It would be difficult to overstate my naïveté when it came to playing music in a professional medical environment. As a volunteer at a hospital in downtown Columbus, my role was simply to play relaxing music in the hallway to create a pleasant ambiance. I was occasionally invited into a room to play a song for a patient, but that was not the norm. I was there simply to provide pretty music in the hallway.

That changed on my first official day as an artist-in-residence. The goal now was to seek meaningful interactions with patients. Jennifer, the art therapist, was my mentor and guide.

"Here's what we'll do. I'll knock on the door of the first two rooms. I'll introduce us and explain what we do. You observe. Depending on the situation, I may ask you to play a song. When we get to the third room, you're on your own."

"OK, fair enough."

Jennifer, a degreed art therapist with years of experience, was very comfortable interacting with patients. She was also a master of the five-second introduction. "Hi, I'm Jennifer the art therapist. Would you like to make something today?" Then she skillfully connected with the patient and/or family to find out if they would like to try a simple art project. Her goal was always to bring something simple and relaxing into what could be a stressful situation.

The first two rooms were easy. Everything went as expected, with a patient in the bed and a family member or two in the room. As the new kid, all I had to do was watch and listen. I may have played a song or two in these rooms; I really can't remember.

Then came door number three. Jennifer looked at the patient info sheet, a daily report with the patient's name and current condition. "This fellow is a frequent flyer." She saw my puzzled look and smiled, "He has a long medical history."

I knocked lightly on the door and cautiously stepped in; she stayed in the hallway. A nurse was on the far side of the room staring at a small machine. A shirtless man was sitting on the bed with a sheet pulled up to his waist. This room was warmer than the first two and there was a different level of intensity. The earlier visits were quiet and relaxed, with patients resting peacefully. In this room, the nurse was intently monitoring the machine which was pushing chemo through tubes attached to the patient. Along with these unfamiliar sights and sounds, a pungent smell filled the room. Everything here was new to me, but not to the patient.

"Hi, my name is John, the artist-in-residence. Would you like to hear some music?"

His response was quick and crisp. "Sure. Folk music. Dylan, Bob Dylan."

I began with "Blowing in the Wind," followed by Gordon Lightfoot's "If You Could Read My Mind," then Peter, Paul and Mary's "Puff the Magic Dragon." As the songs rolled out, the intensity of everything going on in the room was racing in. This was a world away from playing music in a hallway or a casual, "How ya doin'?" hospital visit. This was a face-to-face encounter with a patient actively receiving intense treatment for a very serious disease. How could I expect these simple folk tunes to have any positive impact? There was a rising sense of, *What do you think you are doing here? Music isn't going to help this man.* More songs were requested, and the sense of being overwhelmed ramped up.

Then I heard a different voice. "Stand firm."

I took a closer look around the room. The machine making funny beeps and burps was just a machine. The odor was intense but certainly not fatal; this patient has experienced it many times. Best of all, the man in the bed was genuinely enjoying what he was hearing. Maybe music really does make a difference.

After twenty minutes, I asked, "Would you like to hear anything else?"

"No, that was fine."

When I walked back into the hallway, Jennifer was waiting with a slight smile on her face. Of course, she always had a slight smile on her face, but perhaps this time there was a mischievous glimmer in her eyes. "How did that go?"

"Fine," was my only response.

She acted as if nothing unusual had taken place. In my mind, this was a go/no go test: Can you go into an unfamiliar and challenging situation and calmly do what you are supposed to do, or will you retreat? Interestingly, in all the years of playing music in a medical setting, I have never again experienced this kind of insecurity and doubt.

I've lived long enough to know that when a person begins a new adventure, especially one that holds great potential, there is always pushback. Medieval mapmakers knew something of this when they added the Latin phrase, *Hic sunt dracones*, *"Here be dragons,"* to the unexplored areas of their maps. When you embark on a new adventure, the unknown will stare you in the eye. "Really? You think you can do this? Great danger lies ahead. Hidden reefs and deadly whirlpools await. A wise person would turn back now."

Yes, a wise person might turn back, but not a called person. Onward, ever onward.

"Fly Me to the Moon"

– FRANK SINATRA

I was fourteen years old and cutting the grass on the gentle slope that was my grandparents' front yard. My buddies were riding their two-wheelers up and down our quiet, dead-end street and staring at me. I had no idea why.

After about ten minutes, one of them yelled, "Hey, John, how about a song?"

Unknowingly, I had been singing at the top of my lungs, belting out some Beatles tune to the constant hum of the lawnmower.

In one way or another, music has pushed, pulled, or somehow transported me into almost every interesting event in my life. From pool halls to jails, high school dances to college concerts, from shopping malls to Arts Day with kindergartners, music is what has moved me forward. Ultimately, it took me to the best gig ever, playing music for cancer patients as an artist-in-residence. Put on your dancing shoes, let's step onto the floor of the Radiation/Oncology (Rad/Onc) lobby and see what we find.

* * *

Things are quiet in the waiting room. It has been a busy morning, but for the moment, it is just the admin behind the reception desk and me. I begin playing a lively fingerstyle tune, and I'm about halfway through when in walks a couple, stylishly dressed, probably in their mid-seventies. The man, tall and solid, fit not fat, is in a suit. The perfectly coiffed woman carries a European sense of decorum.

I finish the tune, and he says, "How long have you been playing? One week or two?"

Riffing off his humor, I reply, "A little more than two weeks, but I'm trying to show some improvement every day."

More friendly banter follows. He is a master of lively conversation, an expert in the art of verbal repartee.

"So, let me guess," I venture. "You are either a professional comedian or a pastor."

"No," he replies. "A retired dentist."

"Ahh, your humor reminds me of my Uncle Bob, also a dentist."

They settle in and begin talking together quietly. *Hmmm, what might they enjoy?* Perhaps a little Frank Sinatra. How about an instrumental rendition of "Fly Me to the Moon"?

As I reach the first verse, I notice movement in my peripheral vision. A whirl of color glides past a row of empty chairs. The couple is up and dancing. Not a shuffling, amateur two-step, but a full-on ballroom dance, complete with twirls, spins, dips, and glides. Their movement turns the empty lobby into a grand ballroom.

The moment is transporting. How many times has this couple dazzled friends and family? Certainly, they have been the highlight of many wedding receptions and social gatherings, wordlessly saying,

This is how to move through life: together, unrushed, lovingly, enjoying every moment. Today there are only two witnesses, the admin and me.

The sight is almost too beautiful and too intimate to behold. Stolen glances of a couple facing an unknown future. This is their prelude to a medical consultation, a six-month follow-up after extensive radiation therapy. *Has the treatment worked? How do the numbers look? What should we expect?*

The song ends. The nurse arrives. She invites them down the hall. Together they go, without missing a beat, transitioning from dance steps to footsteps.

Their departure is like waking from a dream.

With a lump in my throat and tears in my eyes, I look across the room.

"Did you see what I just saw?"

"Yes, beautiful."

This is how to move through life, graceful and confident, embracing each moment. A time will come when it is the final dance, but that time is not today.

2

"Good Vibrations"

— THE BEACH BOYS

"Happiness"

– WE BANJOS THREE

Whenever possible, I try to engage people in the next level of musical enjoyment.

Level 1 - Listening

Level 2 - Singing Along

Level 3 - Playing an Instrument

Simply listening to music can engage over 30 areas of our brains, and each new level engages even more neurological connections.

People will often tell me they play—or used to play—an instrument. I invite them to bring their instrument to the next appointment so we can make music together. Sometimes this happens, and it's great! Playing music awakens thoughts and emotions that often remain hidden beneath the surface.

For several weeks, a tall man with an enthusiastic grin always spent a few minutes talking bluegrass music and banjo with me before being called for his radiation treatment.

"Have you heard of this picker? You gotta check out this group!"

He was an exuberant and obvious bluegrass lover. One day, he finally let me in on a not-too-well-hidden secret: He had been playing banjo in a local bluegrass group for over a decade. This enabled me to put a little good-natured pressure on him.

"Dude, you've been holding out on us." ("Us" being me and the other people who had a similar appointment time.)

With a chuckle, he agreed. "OK, OK, I'll bring my banjo next week."

The following week, sure enough, he showed up with the banjo. We had a joyful, impromptu jam session right there in the Rad-Onc lobby.

We started with "Home Sweet Home" and wound our way through a set of bluegrass classics including "Rocky Top," "That Good Ol' Mountain Dew," and "May the Circle Be Unbroken." Our grand finale, by audience request, was "Dueling Banjos." Unlike many pickers who cobble together a few generic banjo licks and "fake" their way through, this fellow knew the right riffs! We pulled off a reasonably respectable rendition that was accompanied by foot stomping, handclapping, and a raucous *Yeehaw!* from our audience.

During our performance a crowd had gathered. Big grins, light hearts, and the sound of strings filled the room. How could anyone not be happy when listening to a lively banjo?

The blend of guitar and banjo generated an impressive new level of energy and excitement. When it comes to pickin' and grinnin', one guitar plus one banjo equals big joy!

"When Irish Eyes are Smiling"

– DR. ARTHUR COLAHAN, POPULARIZED BY BING CROSBY

A gentleman had been coming to radiation treatment for several weeks, a jolly extrovert, tall and distinguished, with plenty of pithy comments and a head full of white hair. He spoke with an accent that sounded vaguely British. During the past several weeks, my schedule was such that we had only exchanged "hellos" in passing, but on this day, our schedules overlapped.

His grown daughter arrived with him. As her father went down the hall for treatment, I asked her what type of music she would enjoy. "Irish," she said and quickly listed a half dozen of her favorite Celtic bands. She mentioned the popular tune "Star of the County Down." It has been covered by many Irish singers, and it's a favorite of mine. We jumped in with that and followed up with two more songs.

As I was playing, her father came back into the lobby. When I finished, he was beaming with a broad smile and bright eyes.

"I'm Irish, and you are singing about places and things that I know," he said.

"Well, if you're Irish, you are surely a good singer. Let's pick out a tune."

His daughter chimed in. "He does have an excellent voice."

He chose "Galway Bay." As expected, he was a melodious Irish tenor and sang this heartfelt song of reminiscence perfectly, capturing every emotional nuance.

Near the end of the song, I noticed his daughter was quietly drying tears. When we finished, I said, "He's a special man, isn't he?" "Yes," she replied, "Yes, he certainly is. He's a great dad."

The following week they were back for his last treatment. As soon as they settled into the lobby, she requested "Galway Bay." Her phone was cued up and ready to capture the performance. Again, the music brought loving tears to her eyes.

The radiation tech arrived and took her dad down the hall for treatment. While he was gone, she explained.

"Mom and Dad used to sing around the house all the time. He grew up near Galway. As a child, I heard 'Galway Bay' more times than I can count; it was one of their favorites. Before last week, I hadn't heard him sing anything in over twenty years, not since right before mom died. To hear him sing that song now..." She trailed off.

The gift of music had enabled her dad to bring the sweetness of the past into the present. A door had been opened to something deeper than physical healing. The lovely melody transported his daughter to the simpler days of youth and tapped into powerful, hidden memories. Is time travel possible? Yes, when music is involved.

"You Are the Sunshine of My Life"

– STEVIE WONDER

A twenty-something Black man curiously leaned out the door of a room on the cancer floor. He grinned,

"Can you play something for my mom?"

When I entered, there was a petite woman, very thin, in the bed. Her cancer appeared to be advanced. She saw the guitar and her beautiful eyes lit up.

"I love the acoustic guitar." The disease had not reduced the radiance of her smile.

Before I had a chance to introduce myself, her son added, "We'd love to hear some music. I'm a musician too." (Interestingly, this was the same hospital room where, a year before, I had played for a grandmother whose grandson was a violinist with the Israel Symphony Orchestra.)

I asked him what instrument he played. Mom proudly replied, "He's a vibe player."

A vibraphone is a large instrument with a magical, bell-like sound. The top has two rows of tone bars arranged like the keyboard of a piano. Under each tone bar is a resonator tube that enhances the sound. Vibes are played with mallets. Experienced players may use one or two mallets in each hand. Originally intended as a novelty instrument in vaudeville, vibes were quickly adopted into the jazz world. Thank you, Lionel Hampton!

The sound is magical, but the instrument is big, bulky, and burdensome. To solve the portability problem, this young man also played the kalimba. A kalimba, aka African thumb piano, uses metal tines on a wooden soundboard to produce music. The soundboard is attached to a gourd, or wooden box, which amplifies the sound. According to Mom, he always has one with him. "As a matter of fact," she said, "he has one with him now." The young man reached into a mid-sized leather backpack and, ta-da! A kalimba!

I asked what style of music they liked. Without hesitation he replied, "Latin jazz."

I had been captured by the music of Antonio Carlos Jobin and other Brazilian guitarist/composers when I was in my teens. It has an optimistic quality with beautifully complex chords and alluring rhythms. Its relaxing yet lively vibe works well in healing environments.

After a small tuning adjustment on my part, I put together a few Brazilian-sounding chords and we jumped into a jam. Though it's much smaller than a vibraphone, this handheld thumb piano makes its own kind of magic. Mom's eyes grew brighter still. Then she closed them as she became totally absorbed in the sound, basking in, drinking in, immersed in the intertwining of kalimba and acoustic guitar.

After about 10 minutes, a doctor entered the room. As I slipped out, Mom's eyes still shining, she gave me one more "Thank you!"

I was able to visit them two more times before she was released to hospice. During our visits, the son told me that because of his mom's illness, he had been sensing a strong calling toward performing healing music. This was the reason for his backpack kalimba and his relentless practicing.

Years ago, he had moved from Columbus to Las Vegas. One day on a crosstown bus ride, he was seated near a father with an unruly kindergarten-aged son. The young boy was crying, causing a ruckus on what was normally a quiet ride.

Wondering if there was something he could do to help, my new friend pulled out his ever-present kalimba and began playing. After a few minutes, the child calmed down and cuddled up next to his dad. The little guy was captivated by the look and sound of this strange instrument.

When the music stopped, a man on the bus said, "Put that thing away. It's distracting."

Immediately the other riders spoke up. “Keep it going!” No doubt, they preferred the sound of a calming kalimba to the caterwauling of a child!

Over the course of my visits, we discussed the whys and whats of my hospital activities. We came up with several ways he could take his music into medical settings.

Years have passed since I met my musical pal, but I’m confident he has found his place, using his magical instruments to bring joy to hurting people. Certainly, his mom is watching from heaven with an even more radiant smile.

“With a Moo Moo Here…”

– TRADITIONAL CHILDREN’S SONG

When I entered the room, Grandma was in the bed, surrounded by children and grandchildren. She asked for “Amazing Grace” and quietly sang along with a verse or two. “Amazing Grace” is truly amazing. People from many different cultural backgrounds relate deeply to this song. Its powerful melody combined with words of hope and forgiveness give it an unmatched universal appeal.

Hospitals can be strange and unfamiliar places for adults, even more so for children. Whenever children are present, I like to treat them to something familiar: “Twinkle, Twinkle Little Star,” “The Alphabet Song,” or “Itsy, Bitsy Spider.” The two young children in this room, probably around four and seven years old, were standing ramrod straight with wide, unblinking eyes. Little Brother had neatly braided cornrows on top of an unexpressive face. Grandma wasn’t looking her best, and the other people in the room were obviously facing a very difficult situation.

I turned to the kids and, with a little chuckle, asked if they had "ever heard this one."

"Old MacDonald had a farm..."

Big Sister began to smile tentatively. Little Brother began to relax. The tension in the room began to ease. By the time we got to the third animal, Little Brother was whispering suggestions to Big Sister. When Sister and I made pig noises, he broke into a huge grin.

The transition from scared little lad to beaming grandson was delightful. I told Grandma that her young grandson had the best-looking smile I'd seen all week. She lit up too. It was easy to see that the young fellow's smile was a gift handed down across the generations.

These simple songs remind us to relax, take a deep breath and live in the present. There have been hard times before, and surely they will come again. We'll make it through with a little music and the help of family and friends.

"Do You Believe in Magic"

– THE LOVIN' SPOONFUL

Cancer doesn't just affect individuals, it impacts families. Adults readily know the seriousness of a cancer diagnosis. They may even have previous experience that prepares them for what may come.

For young children, it's completely different. There is no context, no frame of reference, only questions. Why does Mom feel bad, or why is Dad so sad? Thankfully, children are resilient and often respond with wisdom beyond their years.

A mom who was receiving weekly radiation treatments intentionally scheduled her appointments during morning hours when her son was in school. Today was the first week of Christmas break, so she brought him along.

He was wrapped in a snug winter coat with a red scarf around his neck and a matching knit cap on his head. Being the only child in the waiting room appeared to make him a little fidgety. They sat down close enough to me that we could talk quietly.

Through the large plate glass windows we could see the snow beginning to cover the sidewalk again. I asked if he had plans for sledding today. "Yes, maybe when we get home."

"Are you happy to have a break from school?"

"Yes." As he warmed to the conversation, he looked at my guitar and said, "I sang in the choir at my school's Christmas program last week." He ran down the list of his favorite carols that were part of the concert.

"Would you like to sing something now?" He was surprised and a little nervous but responded with a quick nod of his head, "Can we do 'Silent Night'?"

Without instruction from me, he stood up, walked to the front of the sixty-gallon fish tank, turned and faced a handful of people sitting in small clusters around the lobby. This previously timid young man stood ramrod straight, his neatly combed red hair and freckled face highlighted by the fluorescent glow of the fish tank.

A light strum on the guitar, and he sang with a voice clear and strong, *"Silent night, holy night…"* All conversation stopped. Patients and their family members were captivated by his confidence. (A tip of the hat to vocal teachers everywhere who patiently instruct students to "stand up and sing out.") A few folks quietly joined in.

Our encore was a rousing rendition of "We Wish You a Merry Christmas."

After the figgy pudding verse and one final chorus, this aspiring Ed Sheeran graciously acknowledged the cheers and applause, then sat down beside his beaming mom.

The full-hearted commitment of this young performer spoke to me. The room was unfamiliar, but the act of singing was not. He systematically stepped through several small habits involving posture, position, and presence that won the hearts of his audience. He had a full measure of natural talent. Most importantly, his musical gifting was aimed outward. There was an unspoken sense of *This isn't about me, singing makes my mom happy*. It was a magical moment.

Six months later, I had a magical encounter of a different kind.

It was now summer break, and a thirty-something mom brought her young son along to the radiation lobby. After his mother was seated, he walked over and introduced himself. "Hi, my name is Evan." With a flourish, he handed me his calling card. There, in black and white, the small piece of cardstock proclaimed, "Evan the Magnificent - Magician."

With practiced ease, he reached into his pants pocket, pulled out a deck of playing cards, fanned them in front of me, and boldly, with his ten-year-old voice, recruited me as his assistant. "Pick a card, any card!"

Welcoming his invitation, I chose the three of diamonds. He placed it back in the deck, shuffled, asked me to cut the deck, waved his free hand over the cards, and effortlessly drew the three of diamonds from the pile. That was just the beginning.

Next, he pulled a piece of white cotton rope and a pair of kid's safety scissors from his other pocket. Carefully he cut the rope into two unequal pieces which he tied together. He held the knot tightly, said a few magic words, then opened his hand to reveal the rope in one piece, restored to its original length. From a small black briefcase, his "bag of tricks," he produced a magic box, which he used to make a pencil and a coin disappear and reappear. All this sleight of hand was straight out of a kids' magic book, but his presentation was flawlessly professional, including the cheerful chatter designed to divert and distract. I was impressed. His mother was delighted.

The next week, Evan the Magnificent was back with more tricks. After another stellar performance, his mom told me that Evan had gotten into this hobby a couple of years earlier, about the same time as her diagnosis. Whenever the family went on a trip, he would research the local magic shops and find some new trick or, even better, get a lesson from the shop owner. "He practices at least an hour every day and loves to entertain."

Evan had a knack for entertaining and connecting with his audience. I wouldn't be surprised to see him someday as a lively street performer or perhaps a professional prestidigitator. But, just like his card tricks and engaging chatter, there was much more playing out beneath the surface. Everyone in the lobby enjoyed the show, but there was really only one person in the audience he was aiming to please.

His clever tricks and showmanship,
make sadness disappear.
Presto chango, quick as a wink,
Mom's smiling, bright and clear.
- JDM

Both of these young men intuitively figured out one of the keys to a happy life—giving with an outward focus. Small and insignificant deeds, a song, a trick, become significant when given with love. Love has its own magical way of mysterious multiplication. It can be given away completely with no loss to the giver and absolute gain for the receiver. That's a trick any of us can master.

"Here Comes the Sun"

– THE BEATLES

One October Friday as the leaves were glowing red and gold, my wife and I were exploring Amish Country in northeast Ohio. During lunch, I received a call from a palliative nurse. She asked if I was at the hospital that day.

"No problem," she said. "Contact me on Monday; there is a woman I would like you to visit. She doesn't have a lot of joy in her life right now. The only things that bring her comfort are her pets, which she is away from, and music."

On Monday, the nurse and I connected, and she directed me to a room in the cardiac recovery area. From just outside the door, I observed the attending nurse trying to give the patient some medicine. The nurse was in a kind and caring mood; the patient was in what could be called bulldog mode. She was aggressively expressing her frustration with the medicine, the nurse, and having to be in the hospital.

"You keep giving me that stuff. It's not doing me any good! I want to go home! My pets need me!" She had a dog and multiple cats that her neighbor was tending.

I quietly entered and asked the patient, in the friendliest tone I could muster, "Would you like to hear some music today?"

"Will it stop the pain?" she barked. "All of this is driving me crazy! I miss my pets!"

Again, with a friendly, calm voice, "Some studies have shown that music actually does reduce pain."

Without waiting for a quip or counterpoint, I opened my guitar case and settled into a chair. "What kind of music do you like?"

"Beatles, anything by the Beatles." I mentioned a few titles. She picked "Here Comes the Sun."

When I finished, there was a slight shift in attitude. In a less hostile voice she said, "That was well played. I like the Beatles so much I named my son John. My husband and I were married on John Lennon's birthday." She then went on to enumerate a handful of ways she had woven the Beatles into her life.

Our concert moved on to "Let it Be" and then deeper into the catalogue with "Julia" and "Two of Us." Next, she asked for "Blackbird."

"I saw Paul McCartney when he came to Columbus. When he played 'Blackbird,' everyone cried," she told me.

She had also seen the Beatles at Shea Stadium, one of their first concerts that heralded the "British Invasion." I let her know how impressive it was that she had been part of that pivotal musical moment. "Did you hear any music that day or just screaming?"

"Just screaming." She chuckled. "I still have my ticket." One more Beatles song plus a little musical conversation, then she was ready to rest.

A week later I was invited back. This day, she was not quite cheerful but in a much better mood than our first encounter. Her medical care was moving her metrics in the right direction.

We started with the Beatles but quickly moved to the Eagles and then to Joe Walsh. Joe, the Eagles lead guitar player, is an Ohio boy. She had seen him "hundreds of times, back in the day." Joe's first big group was The James Gang, an extremely popular group during the 60s and early 70s. They made frequent trips from Cleveland to Columbus. This lady had attended almost all those concerts. "Joe is the greatest!"

Reminiscing about the old days brought back loads of pleasant memories of concerts she and her friends had enjoyed. Quoting one of Joe's song titles, she even said, "Life's Been Good to Me So Far." This was a far different woman than the one I had met a week ago!

We got together one more time before she went home. Between the intensive medical care plus a little musical input, this previously tough-shelled patient was now more content and looking to the future. The songs she requested this last time were significantly more optimistic.

Does music ease pain? Can modern medicine move a person from "My life is over" to "God isn't done with me yet"?

Yes, and yes.

"Like a Rolling Stone"

– BOB DYLAN

In my musical life, I've never had the thrill of filling a stadium with adoring fans, but I have experienced the exhilaration of the weird, wild, and wacky that comes with gigging. You never know what may pop up when playing live music in small spaces.

It was Tuesday morning, and I was playing in the lobby of the radiation/oncology area located on the first floor of the medical building. The exterior wall was a series of large plate glass windows facing the parking lot. People inside could see out; people outside could see in.

As I was playing, I noticed a man in the parking lot on his cell phone. He was talking intently and pacing. He would disappear around a corner of the building, then reappear.

I had been watching him for a half an hour when he made his way directly to the Rad/Onc lobby. He sat down beside me and said, "I'm going to ask for a rather strange favor. Can I borrow your guitar?"

I have occasionally let people play my guitar, but I've never had anyone ask to borrow it. When he saw the puzzled look on my face he said, "Look at this."

Phone in hand, he pulled up a picture of a dozen beautiful electric guitars carefully lined up on guitar stands in a well-appointed music room. "I just want you to see that I have a great deal of respect and appreciation for beautiful guitars." He went on, "My daughter is in labor in the main medical building next door. She just received an epidural. I would like to make a short video of me playing 'Comfortably Numb.'"

OK, now I was linking up with this dad's sense of humor and love for his daughter. I asked, "Would you like me to shoot the video?"

"That would be fantastic!"

I swapped my guitar for his phone. He began playing the intro to Pink Floyd's classic song and I began recording. When he finished, he said, "I'm kind of a rookie player, but she'll get a kick out of this."

We swapped back. Grinning from ear to ear, he said, "Thanks, this is amazing!"

About 10 minutes later, he came back into the lobby and said, "Uhh, could I ask another favor? Could you shoot that video again and hold the phone horizontally?"

"Sure, no problem. Take Two!" We made our second music video, this time for the big screen.

When he finished, he asked if I had another minute. He pulled up the picture of the beautiful guitars again.

"These guitars are the exact models and years of the guitars that Keith Richards played for the Rolling Stones' biggest hits." He went through each guitar, pointing and connecting: "Satisfaction," "Honky Tonk Women," "Wild Horses," "Brown Sugar," right on down the line, explaining all the fine details, including the model number and the year each instrument was built. "This one is tuned to Open G with the low E string removed." The collection was worth a small fortune. It was truly a mind-blowing, totally obsessive, fan-geek assembly of stellar instruments.

"I think you qualify as a super fan!"

"I live in Connecticut; Keith Richards is one of my neighbors." Pointing out the window, he said, "He lives about as far away from me as that Kroger store" (a few hundred feet away).

"So, you hang out with Keith Richards!"

"No, no, he doesn't know me from a piece of shoe leather, but occasionally we wave at each other. I'll tell you a funny story. I have a young friend who was just learning to play the guitar. He is a huge Stones fan too. There's a dingy little bar in our neighborhood that has an open mic on Wednesdays. With some encouragement from me, my friend signed up for it. He got on stage and announced that he was going to play 'Honky Tonk Women.' He was in standard tuning and began playing a decent rendition of the introduction. Suddenly, from the back of the room a voice yelled, 'What the @h#$ are you doing? That's not how you play that song!' The crowd was aghast. Out of the shadows stepped Keith Richards. He proceeded to the stage and, in a very friendly way, took the guitar, re-tuned it to an Open G tuning, and showed my friend the right way to play the song. Needless to say, the crowd went wild, and my friend was over the moon."

His cell phone rang. He answered, "I'll be right there." He turned back to me, thanked me again, and said, "Baby's coming!" He was gone in a "Jumpin' Jack Flash."

I've never filled a stadium, but I've met a guy who knows a guy who had an on-stage guitar lesson with a genuine rock star who has filled lots of stadiums!

"Sing Me Back Home"

– MERLE HAGGARD

It was near the end of my day on the cancer floor. I knocked on the door of a room near the south nurses' station, and inside was a woman standing by herself. She was wearing a somber expression and dressed in a hospital gown that she barely filled.

"Hi, I'm John, the artist-in-residence. Would you like to hear some music?"

She looked up. "Yes. I just received some very bad news from the doctor."

She sat down on the bed slowly and pulled up the covers. I began playing "Diamonds in the Snow," a gentle, relaxing tune from my first CD. After about 20 seconds, there was a little cough, a little throat clearing.

"Do you like this song?"

"Yes, it's fine, but do you have something with more of a beat to it? Something country?"

"How about Johnny Cash, 'Folsom Prison Blues'?" It was early in my time at the hospital, and fortunately I had memorized all the lyrics to this country classic.

"That would be great!"

I jumped into this iconic song, and before I knew it, her toes were tapping underneath the bed sheet. She was smiling and quietly clapping her hands.

When I finished, she said, "That takes me back. Years ago, I was a cook at Leavenworth penitentiary out there in Kansas. The prisoners used to call me Cookie. There were some very rough guys there who had done terrible things, but they always treated me nice. If ever there was trouble in the cafeteria, they would watch out for me and always keep me safe. When there was a fight, two or three big guys would stand around me and make sure I was okay. They always took good care of me."

Johnny's classic prison song had unlocked the door to a storehouse of memories. Good memories that brought tears. We covered a few more outlaw tunes, and in between, she told me stories of unlikely friendships in unlikely places with unlikely people—bad people who still had some good to offer. "I don't believe that anyone is all bad," she said. There were more tears punctuated by a few chuckles.

Music had transported Cookie from bad news in a hospital room to brighter times in a dark place.

– GENESIS

The automatic doors to the Rad/Onc lobby swooshed opened with a frigid blast of December wind. In walked a woman wearing navy blue scrubs. According to the hospital's "Color Code for Caregivers," this indicated that she was a nurse. She was pushing a transport chair.

The person in the chair was more difficult to discern. His hair was a brown, bushy, wild, and wiry bird's nest. On his face, the bird's nest became a scruffy profusion of facial hair. His eyes were tightly shut; I would find out later this was due to blindness. His body twisted to the right, adjusting and readjusting, fretfully looking for a comfortable position, unable to sit up straight. There were no words from his mouth, only moans, groans, and grunts.

Sadly, this man was suffering with many serious physical and mental limitations. On top of that was whatever medical condition had brought him to this waiting room. His attending nurse rolled him to the admin desk for check-in, then parked his transport chair in a spot next to a row of patient chairs. She sat down beside him.

A continuous flow of song requests had made this a delightfully musical morning. There had been songs ranging from Johnny Cash to Frank Sinatra, with a heapin' helpin' of Beatles and James Taylor. Our new arrival was a significant departure from the regular crowd. What kind of music would speak to him? I walked over to his nurse and asked.

"He's deaf."

My role at the hospital was to use sound to relax patients as they enter a new and potentially stressful situation. This day's challenge was how to use sound to calm a person who was blind, deaf, and incapable of speech.

I remembered the story of Helen Keller. She overcame similar handicaps with the help of her teacher and lifelong friend, Anne Sullivan. Anne initially taught Helen vocabulary using touch. With her fingers, she would write words on Helen's palm.

I moved to the left side of the patient and took his right hand, placing his fingers firmly on the soundboard of my guitar. Then I began to play slowly and melodically.

His demeanor changed instantly; his eyebrows shot up while his eyes remained shut. A long series of loud "ooooh, ooooh, ooochs" replaced the grunts and groans. After this initial startle, he quit fidgeting and started making cooing sounds. We continued this fingertip concert for about five minutes until he was called for his treatment.

Human brains exhibit a high degree of plasticity. That bundle of neurons between our ears can change and adapt its structure to improve its efficiency. For example, the area of a blind person's brain that would normally process sight can rewire itself, so to speak, to benefit one of the other senses, perhaps enabling an increased sensitivity to touch.

Oh, to know what was going through this man's mind as he felt those musical vibrations. Was he able to hear through the sensations in his fingertips? Science says, yes. Studies have shown that deaf people can and do experience music. They are able to feel tone, pitch, volume, and the quality (timbre) of sound even if they can't hear it.

I don't know how it all works, but I know that something happened that day in the waiting room. Music crossed the bridge to the lonely island of this man's inner world.

"Hit Me With Your Best Shot"

– PAT BENATAR

One morning at the infusion center, a nurse invited me into a room where a patient was getting settled into bed. Her husband was seated beside her. She appeared to be nervous and apprehensive during the pre-treatment prep.

The nurse introduced me to the couple then said, "This is her first treatment. She's a little nervous. Could you play something for her?"

The wife told me she and her husband were both big John Denver fans. They had recently watched a Public Broadcasting special about his life. It reminded them of how much they loved his music. Considering that "Country Roads" is my second-most requested song, this was a simple enough assignment. Every guitarist of a certain age knows this universal campfire song.

"Almost heaven ..." For three minutes and ten seconds we each became honorary West Virginians.

There was toe tapping under the sheets, quiet singing on the chorus, and a noticeable relaxation of the shoulders. By the end of the song there appeared the hint of a smile.

When we finished the last chorus, the nurse came back into the room. I was standing by the bedside, inadvertently blocking her access to the infusion pump. I stepped to the side.

"If I'm in your way, just let me know."

"No problem," she replied. "I was just waiting for you to finish your song. Now I need to give her a shot for nausea."

I let that statement hang in the air for a second, then gave the nurse a quizzical look. It was my turn to smile. *I played a song and now the patient needs a shot for nausea!*

"Can you come to all my gigs?"

The mental image of a nurse injecting anti-nausea medication at a concert made its way around the room. Smiles and laughter eased the patient into her first treatment with a lighter heart—and no nausea.

"We Are Family"

– SISTER SLEDGE

I met her on a Wednesday. Let's call her "Shirley." She invited me into a room where her sister was in the bed, unresponsive.

Shirley was a sweet, short Black woman with a delightful smile. She and her husband had been traveling from North Carolina to a midwestern state for a church conference when they got the call that Shirley's sister had been admitted to the hospital. They quickly rerouted their trip and came straight to Columbus. When they arrived at the hospital, her sister was unresponsive.

Shirley was a woman of strong faith. We talked about what the nurses had told her: Keep talking to your sister, even when she does not respond; hearing is the last of the senses to go. She can still hear you.

Shirley and her sister loved church music so we quickly settled on some of her sister's favorite hymns. I sang, and Shirley joined in quietly on parts of the choruses. I could tell she had a good voice. When I asked her if she was in a choir, she said, "Yes, but that was a long time ago." Even so, I encouraged her to sing. We had a nice visit that lasted about fifteen minutes.

The following Monday when I was back on the floor, she told me the doctor had just informed them that her sister had days, maybe hours, left. We had a brief visit in the hall. She was busy contacting relatives regarding this sad news.

Two days later, to my surprise, Shirley found me as she was "getting her steps in" by walking laps around the floor. We went back to her sister's room. Shirley's husband was sitting on the couch, studying a large textbook. He welcomed me with a friendly fist bump. Her sister didn't appear to have moved since our first meeting. This time, I noticed she was wrapped in a snug flannel blanket that was completely covered with family photos, some large, some small, all printed directly onto the fabric. This woman was literally covered by her loving family. At the foot of the bed were two throw pillows with even more photos. I asked for a "tour."

Shirley smoothed the blanket and began.

"This is a picture of the full family, Mommy, Daddy, four sisters, and three brothers. The children were always arranged in age order, oldest to youngest." Shirley and her sister were now the last two surviving siblings.

Mommy was a committed Christian, and before breakfast and after dinner, the children had worship time. Every day of their growing up years was bracketed by hymn singing. As the children got older, they would take turns choosing and leading the songs. Daddy supported Mommy completely. "He wasn't as spiritual as Mommy, but he fully supported her."

Daddy was a worker and a miracle. He was born with a serious heart condition. Doctors said he was unlikely to live more than a year. They asked the family to leave the boy with the hospital so that they could study his condition, code words for conducting research on him. His mother had adamantly refused. "He is our child, and we will raise him by God's grace." This child lived into his 70s, was the head of a large family, and was known throughout the community for his work ethic. In addition to his job, he planted an acre-and-a-half family garden every year. The garden produced fresh vegetables for healthy bodies and planted the lessons of labor in each child.

She continued with stories of nieces and nephews, aunts and uncles. "This is a wedding picture... That was a birthday." Each picture sparked a story, lovingly told.

One story that especially moved me was of her nephew. He was a young man who spent his too-short life committed to always doing the right thing. During his time at Ohio Wesleyan University, he was involved in lots of campus activities and was everyone's best friend. He loved to sing and started several choirs with people of every race and background. When he came back for his 10-year class reunion he and a friend were on his motorcycle. As they were riding, a car suddenly crossed in front of them. The nephew was killed. The last act of his life was to intentionally push his friend backward, a move that saved his friend's life. The line for his memorial service at the university's Gray Chapel stretched around the block. The service itself was four hours long because so many friends wanted to share the significant ways that he had touched their lives.

There were many other outstanding family stories of love and service. In their early days, Shirley and her husband had been missionaries for eight years overseeing a leper hospital in Sri Lanka.

After the blanket tour, she asked for several classic hymns, "In the Garden," "Blessed Assurance," and "How Great Thou Art." During our first meeting, she sang only a little and very quietly. On this day, she let her soprano voice ring out. It was a grateful voice brought to life by her rich family history. As expected, she knew every word to every verse of every hymn. Years of twice-daily hymn singing will do that for a person.

In the middle of our singing, Shirley remembered that I had just missed connecting with one of her nieces on my first visit. After that visit, she had told her niece about "this guy who stopped by with a guitar."

"My goodness, is he still doing that?" It turned out her niece was a lady I knew from the hospital and church. She had worked in the oncology department of this hospital when I was just beginning my artist-in-residence role. She was still working in the oncology world but now had moved to another large Ohio city. Shirley quickly got her on the phone, and we were able to catch up. It was one more example of the puzzle pieces of life coming together.

One of the unexpected gifts that music has given me, especially in this role, is a window into the lives of people I would otherwise never know. Even though it is a tragic illness that brings us together, there is comfort in seeing how we are all woven into the huge tapestry of life with multiple points of intersection.

My visit with Shirley provided a micro view. She had beautifully explained, *This is my family. This is who we are and what we've done.* Her sister was literally wrapped in a legacy of love, faith, and purpose.

"Carry On Wayward Son"

– KANSAS

Thursday had been a long, tiring day. Believe it or not, sometimes playing guitar for five or six hours a day can start to feel like work. I was more than ready to head home to a nice supper. Leaving the hospital five or ten minutes later than normal could mean the difference between a quick half-hour ride home or an undetermined amount of time sitting on an expressway disguised as a parking lot. I was almost to the elevator when I saw Howard, a friend.

We had met years before when he was recruited to be part of a string quartet that would provide a little extra sparkle to a series of Christmas services. He played violin, I played guitar, and somehow, we ended up sitting beside each other. We had fun hanging out between services. A few weeks later, I invited him to my house to jam. He brought his violin and some foot pedals. We had an enjoyable morning making music and experimenting with his pedals. Howard was a worship leader at a small church northwest of Columbus. Not long after we met, he moved to one of the Carolinas. I hadn't seen him since the move.

What a surprise to see him now and have a chance to get caught up. The move had been good for him, and his life was going well. Of course, meeting a friend on the cancer floor is bittersweet.

"Good to see you. What brings you here?" I asked him.

He replied, "A friend from my old church is on this floor. She's going through some rough things. I was in town, so I told her I would stop by and play a little music."

"Well," I said, "unless you have a fiddle or guitar in your back pocket, I don't see what you're going to be playing that music on."

He laughed. "I didn't know she was in the hospital till I got in town. I didn't bring any instruments on this trip."

I handed him my guitar. "This may be of some use to you."

We went down the hall and found the room. His friend was there, and so were a half dozen other folks. This was pre-COVID, with no limit on visitors in the room. Word had gotten out that Howard would be stopping by, and old friends were eager to see and hear him. It was a warm and joyous reunion.

As folks settled in, Howard opened the guitar case and began with a favorite worship song. There was quiet singing as he masterfully brought the room into a peaceful unity. We all basked in his musical gift for the next twenty minutes.

My role? I hadn't played a note or said a word beyond "hello." I just happened to be the pack horse, carrying the gear, steadily clomping forward on uncharted trails. Lives intersect, the gear arrives on time and intact, musical magic happens.

Was I late for dinner? Not enough to worry about.

"Good Old Mountain Dew"

– THE STANLEY BROTHERS

At times it can be tricky to figure out who is who in a patient's room. How do these human puzzle pieces fit together? The young man sitting on the couch may be a son or a nephew or a neighbor. The middle-aged lady in the chair could be a niece or a daughter. The man standing by the window could be a husband or even an ex-husband.

What about that person quietly reading a book by the bed? Hmm, that mystery person might be a patient sitter. Sitters are trained medical professionals who provide constant one-on-one bedside observation. A variety of situations may require this level of care: fall risks, psychological issues, or the possibility of self-harm. Sitters are present to respond quickly if needed. Fortunately, the patient is often resting or sleeping, and this allows time for the sitter to read while staying on watch.

When I entered the room, a fellow a little older than me was in the bed. He was resting but not asleep. An attractive young woman, dressed in plain clothes that looked like scrubs, was sitting by the bed reading. She didn't look up.

I introduced myself to the man. When I asked what he would like to hear, he said, "Anything country." He turned toward the woman and said, "Play something lively that she can dance to. Come on, baby, you'll dance for me, won't you?"

She smiled politely and brushed off the invitation without a word.

He named an upbeat country tune, and we were off and running. She remained stone-still, engrossed in her book.

When I finished, he said, "I've got to tell you a funny story. When I was in Nam, I was in a company with this white guy who received a wedding cake. There we are in camp, and he gets this huge wedding cake. I ask him, 'What's going on with that?' He tells me he is the son of country music star Buck Owens, and that Buck had recently gotten married. To celebrate, Buck sent him this wedding cake. Then he tells me when he gets out of the service, he is going to play drums for Buck and make all kinds of big money on a new TV show called *Hee Haw*. I tell him that can't be true, since country bands at that time didn't have drummers. But sure enough, two years later, he got me tickets to the show. I went backstage and met all kinds of country stars.

"You see, I grew up in the mountains of Virginia, and before I got into the service, I never heard anything but country music. All the other Black guys in my company were into Motown. When they found out I'd never heard of Motown, they called me every name in the book. But I knew plenty about country music. That helped me connect with Buck's son."

As he was speaking, a nurse came in to draw blood. As part of the procedure, she asked him for his birth date. He responded with a date indicating he was born in the late 1940s, then said, "But I told her,"—nodding toward the sitter—"I was born in '68."

She gave him a look, then back to the book.

He asked for "Country Roads" and sang along. Then another story.

"Growing up in the mountains of Virginia was pretty tough. My dad was a moonshiner and worked me like crazy helping out. I couldn't wait to get out of there. Moonshining's hard work. My dad had a regular job too.

"One time he got arrested for moonshining. They locked him up and we didn't expect to have him back anytime soon. The welfare people came out to the house and asked my mom how many children she had. She said seven. They said, 'That's a lot of kids.' She told them, 'I've got more than seven. I thought you just meant the ones in elementary school.' When the welfare folks found out how many kids and how much it was going to cost the welfare agency to take care of them, they went back to the judge. The judge let Dad out after four days. He told Dad, 'You go back to what you were doing so you can take care of all those kids.'

"But while Dad was gone, Mom got a boyfriend. Like I said, nobody was expecting Dad back any time soon. The boyfriend was a big guy, but when he saw Dad coming, he about tore a hole in the side of that little shotgun house, getting out of there. You see, Dad was a big guy too."

Naturally, that story called for a rendition of George Jones's tune, "White Lightning."

When I finished, the reader finally spoke up. "You know, this is the first time that he's smiled since we've been here." Singing about the Blue Ridge Mountains, reminiscing, and singing about moonshining had cheered him up.

Turns out he and the sitter—his wife—had just traveled through the Blue Ridge Mountains a few weeks prior.

"She's from Slovakia," he told me. "She speaks six languages. When we first met, I told her I could teach her to speak English. She said, 'I can't even understand what you are saying; the words you are using aren't even real English.' See, she had learned the Queen's English. She didn't have any idea how to speak hillbilly. That was our first disagreement. She won."

From there, the conversation went to language, music, and the way they connect to each other. He also talked about the way music and language connect us to each other. "Those country songs tell a lot of stories. They really give you a window into someone else's world.

"You know, I didn't know anything but country music in Nam, but that helped me understand some of the white guys in my company. The music today, that rap, breaks people apart instead of bringing people together. You know, you shouldn't even say the n-word these days, but they say it all the time. It's no wonder people are fighting and killing each other. You listen to that stuff, and it gets to you. Music is supposed to bring us together not tear us apart."

Well said, my friend, well said.

"This Land is Your Land"

– WOODY GUTHRIE

One Tuesday, a couple walked into the Rad-Onc lobby. The man was dressed in a green army jacket with numerous veteran patches covering the shoulders and sleeves. He was a wiry fellow, quiet but not unfriendly, sporting a thin mustache and eyes that were intense and wary.

His wife was the talkative one. She told me he enjoyed music and used to play the harmonica. “Actually, he is still very good on the harmonica,” she said.

They requested a few classic country songs, Willie Nelson, Johnny Cash, and Merle Haggard. In between tunes, I mentioned that it would be very cool if, on his next appointment, he brought a harmonica so we could play together. Still reserved, he replied, “I’ll think about it.”

When they arrived the following week, he pulled out a harmonica. We started to play but before we got far, he was called for his treatment. As he headed down the hall, he said, “Maybe I can stay for a minute when I’m done with this.”

When he came back to the lobby, he unloaded the contents of his multi-pocketed jacket. He hadn’t brought just one harmonica; by the time he worked his way through every pocket there were a half dozen more laid out on the table between us.

I was expecting a wailing blues riff; instead, he asked, “Do you know ‘Turkey in the Straw’?” We jumped right in. He had a good ear and powerful tone. As soon as we finished, without a word he started in to “Red River Valley.” Next was “You are My Sunshine.” He seemed slightly winded after each song but kept the music flowing.

When he was ready for a break, he said, “My respiratory therapist is going to be happy to hear I’m doing this.”

I asked where he learned to play so well. “I was a soldier in Vietnam. In the evenings, things would settle down a little and I would play. The guys would sit around the fire and listen.”

What a picture: battle-weary young men, eighteen to twenty years old, halfway around the world, listening to traditional American folk music and thinking of home. He went on to tell me that his first bout with cancer had occurred 10 years ago. "Probably exposure to Agent Orange."

We resumed our concert, with him changing out harmonicas as we traveled through a variety of keys. Yes, he had come ready to "stay for a minute"—and about 29 more minutes after that. The intensity of his eyes softened as we continued through more folk tunes, some he knew and some he didn't. It made no difference; in either case, he would catch on quickly and come up with something that sounded great. As we dug deeper into these traditional melodies, he was transported, connected to the world of sound and rhythm.

What makes a great musical performance? Is it the perfect venue with a great sound system, creative lighting, and a huge audience hanging on every note? For this performance, there was none of that, just a man emotionally committed to sending his life's breath over the reeds of a simple instrument. He was breathing in, breathing out; wind from damaged lungs releasing sound from a place of deep memories, dreams, and nightmares. He had experienced years of PTSD (post-traumatic stress disorder).

As we played, there was a strong grounding in the present. How many breaths still reside in these lungs? How many moments until the final exhale? His performance said, "All I know is that I have this moment."

Over the next weeks, we were able to play together four more times. He grew weaker toward the end of his treatment.

For me, each session was a humbling experience as I saw how these simple folk tunes brought such comfort and relief, recalling the best of memories from the worst of times. What a privilege to make music with this noble soldier, a soldier once again in a battle for his life.

"War (What is it Good For?)"

– EDWIN STAR

History is more than the dates and facts we learn in school. History is lived by people. I have met tottering old men who were once young soldiers on the beaches of Normandy and middle-aged men who were part of Desert Storm. On this day, I encountered a young man who had survived a significant historical event when he was just a child.

An infusion area is a busy place, so I don't expect to hear much applause when I play. When I do, it piques my curiosity. As I finished "Carolina in My Mind," hand clapping from a nearby infusion bay reached my ears. I peeked in. Sitting in the infusion chair was an Asian fellow grinning from ear to ear.

"I really like that song," he said, then invited me to have a seat.

I try to be sensitive in following the verbal and non-verbal cues of a patient, to see where the conversation should go. Sometimes it's light and friendly, other times it's a deep dive. On this day, music opened the door to a personal story that took place during one of the darker chapters of America's history. Here's what he told me.

Hao narrowly escaped from Vietnam when he was six years old. Up to that point, he had lived a relatively normal, middle-class life. Suddenly everything changed forever.

In April of 1975, Vietnam was plunged into chaos as the communist North Vietnamese army came flooding into Saigon. Hao's father, an officer in the South Vietnamese army, was working with the American troops and in grave danger. While others were fleeing, he volunteered to stay behind with his troops. To the best of his ability, he gave his family directions for safe passage out of the country. "Go to the airport."

Hao, his mother, and two aunts immediately fled. They were met with pandemonium at the tarmac. Crowds of screaming and frightened people were clinging to and falling from the wings and wheel wells of the airplanes attempting takeoff.

Amid this confusion, Hao's mother spotted a van marked "US State Department." They ran toward it. Fortunately, a Marine saw them and cleared the way. The van was overloaded with men fearing for their lives.

"Families first!" the Marine bellowed. With the help of the driver and another Marine, he grabbed the men and forcefully pulled them from the vehicle. Hao and his relatives were stuffed in, along with other frightened women and children. The doors slammed shut. They sped down the road to a barge waiting on the Saigon River.

The cargo hold of the barge was filled with terrified women and crying children. More were pouring in by the minute. Sandbags stacked ten high lined the perimeter of the deck. A tugboat arrived, hitched its towlines, and began pulling the barge toward the mouth of the river. Before they reached open water, a torrent of machine gun and shoulder-launched grenades came zinging in from the shore. Tracer bullets hit the sandbags, and grenades sent sandbags tumbling onto the whimpering children below.

At sunset, the barge, still under fire, miraculously made it as far as the mouth of the river. Without warning, the tugboat decoupled and vanished into the twilight, leaving the helpless evacuees stranded. A half hour later, a US battleship pulled alongside and shone its blinding spotlight into the hold—then disappeared into the rapidly fading light.

Within twenty minutes, the tugboat reappeared, re-coupled, and pulled the barge to deep water where the refugees were transferred to the battleship, then to an aircraft carrier and onward to the Philippines.

Fast forward fifteen years to a classroom at The Ohio State University. As part of a lecture on the Vietnam War, Hao's history professor, a retired Navy officer, described his part in that exact rescue mission. At the end of the lecture, Hao held up his hand. "I was on that barge."

The professor replied, "Come to my office after class."

When Hao arrived, they dug into the details of that horrendous day. Mid-conversation, the professor said, "Just a minute." He picked up his phone and began to dial. On the other end of the line, the battleship commander, still active in the Navy, answered.

Hao, full of emotion, thanked the commander for saving his life and the lives of the other children. As their conversation continued, the commander said, "One thing you don't know—the Navy hired that Japanese tugboat to pull the barge to safety in deep water. When the tugboat came under fire, they cut and ran. Once we verified who was in that barge, it didn't take long to track down the tug. I had to threaten them with a torpedo to get them to go back."

Even as a six-year-old, Hao was thrilled when he finally arrived in America though he knew nothing of the language or the culture. He picked up English quickly, mostly by watching television. As soon as he learned to read English, he became a regular patron of the library, delighted to check out as many books as his young arms could carry.

After high school, he earned degrees in history and journalism, then successfully made his mark in the business world. His cancer had forced him to step down from his career, but now he was serving as a volunteer teaching ESL (English as a Second Language) classes at a large community center in Westerville.

Over the years, I have had the privilege of meeting many veterans, but this was the first time I had an in-depth conversation with one of the beneficiaries of their bravery. Many of the stories born out of the war in Vietnam are tragic. The loss of lives, the civil unrest at home, and the way Vietnam veterans were treated upon their return are all part of this sad chapter. I felt privileged and grateful to listen to Hao's story of rescue and all he had done as an American citizen.

Incredibly, the currents flowing through the river of life had brought together this former refugee and two of his rescuers.

War – what is it good for? The song says, "absolutely nothing!" Yet redemption can come from even the deepest of tragedies.

"Wasting Away in Quarantinaville"

– JIMMY BUFFET PARODIES BY VARIOUS YOUTUBERS

And then there was COVID...

In March of 2020, everything changed. Businesses shut down, people stayed home, and a mixture of malaise and paranoia settled over the land. No one knew what this strange and unexpected virus was capable of.

Fortunately, the health care system that I worked for was committed to a no-layoff policy. We couldn't work with patients the way we normally did, so this meant redeployment. Many nurses, techs, and one musician were redeployed as temperature checkers.

There were always two people assigned to each entrance of the cancer center. My new, self-titled work position was Assistant Thermometer Operator. All my temp check partners were medical professionals, so I mentally promoted them to Chief Thermometer Operators.

The training for this position took approximately 3 minutes: Here's your thermometer, push this button, run the sensor across the person's forehead, take note of their temperature. If it's too high, they need to contact their doctor. Lastly, give every person whose temperature is within the healthy range a hospital-approved mask.

We were instructed to occasionally wipe down the handrails and elevator buttons and anything else people touched. A week later, we received upgraded thermometers which simplified the process: Place the sensor close to the person's forehead, push the button, read the temperature.

Aside from occasional slow times toward the end of the day, this was an enjoyable experience. Way better than sitting at home unpaid! A big plus was the opportunity to meet folks from departments that I don't normally visit. Getting a bigger picture of what goes on in the hospital was interesting and educational.

Even more interesting were the people. Some of my rotating colleagues used our downtimes to read and study. Others, like the nurse with extensive European travel experience, were great conversationalists. My favorite day was spent with a fellow who normally worked in cardiology. He was born and raised in Zambia. Our wide-ranging conversation was like a college-level class on the history and culture of Africa, complete with further reading assignments!

All in all, being an Assistant Thermometer Operator was an easy gig. The medical people coming through our entrance were key workers taking care of critical patients. They were professionals who understood the need for this minor inconvenience and handled it good-naturedly. The non-medical people coming through our entrance were mainly cancer patients with compromised immune systems. They understood this little ritual was for their protection. But not everyone appreciated the precautions being taken.

One man, reporting for his first day of chemotherapy, saw the fifteen-second temperature check as an invasion of his personal privacy. In all fairness, the first day of chemo can be a stressor for anyone. Still, his reaction was a little over-the-top. "Why are you taking my temperature? I can't believe I'm being subjected to this! You're all stooges of the government!"

To say he was irritated would be a serious understatement. Everything about this fellow's demeanor said, "Leave me alone!" Tufts of shaggy, white hair poked in every direction from under his weathered baseball cap. His denim coat and pants were tattered and worn; his t-shirt stained. His tall, thin frame reminded me of a walking scarecrow. There was no hint of any civilizing female influence in his appearance. One could easily picture him as the cranky neighbor yelling, "You kids get off of my lawn!"

He made it through the ordeal then angrily marched off toward the elevator. During my temperature-taking days, he was the only person who ever raised an objection.

After nine weeks, I was able to resume playing guitar for patients, but no singing, not even with a mask. Over the next year and a half, I saw this gentleman at regular intervals. He would say "Hi" on his way into an infusion bay. His mode of dress remained the same, but he was now visibly calmer. Good nurses will do that for a person.

One day, after months of "hi's" and head nods, he called me over to his infusion bay. I had no idea if he remembered our first encounter.

"Did I hear you just play a B.B. King riff in that last song?" he asked.

I assured him that I followed the time-honored tradition of stealing great riffs wherever I could find them, and yes, that would include anything I could borrow/steal from B.B. King.

He invited me to sit down and asked, "Do you remember the Agora?"

The Agora was a legendary rock music venue located on High Street across from the Ohio State University Student Union. In 1984, it was renamed the Newport Music Hall and remains a must-play venue for up-and-coming rock bands. It is the longest continuously running rock club in the country, going strong for over fifty years.

"Yes," I replied. "I heard Dave Workman there in 1970."

The conversation flowed. "I heard so many great concerts there back in the '70s." He continued with tales of favorite artists he had heard live when they were still unknown: Neil Young, Todd Rundgren, B.B. King, Joe Walsh, and more. We had plenty of common ground in our musical tastes and spent about thirty minutes reminiscing like two old friends comparing record collections.

If I had to guess, I would say he did remember our first encounter. He was now a different man, calm and reflective. He thanked me for "all the music" I had played during his treatment. "You know," he continued, "I was always listening for the times you would throw in bits and pieces of songs that I knew. The music really makes all of this better." I didn't know it then, but that was his last treatment and the last time I would see him.

Small things had made the difference. Bits and pieces of favorite songs, empathetic medical care, time for reflection, and a half-hour conversation had transformed "cranky guy" into a friend.

"Ring My Bell"

– ANITA WARD

Cancer isn't an easy disease. Chemotherapy and radiation therapy aren't easy treatments. Both take time. Chemo can stretch into regular infusions over weeks or even years. Radiation treatment is short and long: fifteen-minute daily treatments spread over five to eight weeks. Many patients experience a combination of both. Each method comes with significant side effects.

Perseverance pays off, but that doesn't make it easy. Treading this path is a rugged hike, not a walk around the block. To mark the completion of treatment, some cancer centers offer a small but significant celebration—ringing the bell. This tradition began in 1996 at MD Anderson Cancer Center in Houston, Texas, when Admiral Irve Le Moyne introduced a Navy tradition, ringing a bell for a job well done, into the medical world. It quickly caught on at other medical facilities.

The bell may be handheld or wall mounted. Nurses and techs, families and friends, companions on the journey, gather around. The method of ringing varies from person to person. For some, a simple *ding* is sufficient; for others, it's the clatter of a five-alarm fire. I've seen many types of bell celebrations, from a spouse shooting a brief video to a pop-up family reunion, complete with kids, grandkids, and great grandkids carrying balloons and cake.

Whatever the manner of celebration, the result of the ringing is much the same: hugs, tears, best wishes, and cheers. Chapter closed; a milestone reached.

"Stand by Me"

– BEN E. KING

There is a rhythm to the flow of people in a Radiation waiting room. The patient arrives ten or fifteen minutes before their scheduled appointment, often accompanied by a friend or family member. They check in, then sit and wait to be called for treatment.

One morning when I arrived, there was a fellow sitting in the back corner of the waiting room. Fifteen, thirty, sixty minutes later, he was still there. He would occasionally speak to the folks who were coming and going, but mostly he kept to himself. As it turned out, he was there for over two hours.

As I was getting ready to leave, I walked over and told him that he had me baffled. I had never seen anyone hang out in a waiting room for so long. With a smile, I asked, "Who are you and what are you up to?"

He laughed. "I'm a driver. I take people to their medical appointments. This has been an interesting morning," he went on. "I spend a lot of time in waiting rooms, but not usually as long as today. These places can be very depressing; no one talks, people are alone with their thoughts. But this place is different. What you are doing with the music really brightens things up. People are more relaxed, they're talking to each other, and there's a sense of hope."

Music can break down the walls of lonely silence. It's something that gives strangers a point of connection that has nothing to do with disease. I've observed casual waiting room connections grow into informal support groups. Radiation treatment five days a week for multiple weeks is particularly conducive to this.

I remember one group of three men who had consecutive fifteen-minute treatment schedules. They were from different generations but going through the same experience. The first man, in his late thirties, arrived at 8:00; the second, in his mid-sixties, came at 8:15; and the third, in his mid-forties, at 8:30.

Music was the conversation starter for them. The older gentleman took the initiative in getting to know the other fellows. Soon the three of them were waiting till they had all received their daily dose of radiation then, like old friends, went to breakfast at a local diner.

After several weeks, Mr. 8:00 and Mr. 8:15 completed their treatment, but they still all continued to meet at the diner for breakfast. The youngest of the trio was the last to complete his treatment. To his surprise and delight, his two new friends made it a point to be in the Radiation lobby when he rang the bell. The three former strangers were laughing, hugging, and back-slapping like their football team that just won the Super Bowl. They celebrated the morning by treating him to a nice breakfast at a classier place than their usual greasy spoon.

How do you convert a stranger to a friend? It starts with "Hello."

3

"I Never Promised You a Rose Garden"

— LYNN ANDERSON

"You're So Vain"

– CARLY SIMON

Pre-COVID, I was asked to make brief presentations to nurses participating in quarterly palliative care training classes. Preparation for this was an opportunity to review interactions that had taken place in recent weeks or months. There are always fresh stories of how music has made a positive difference in a patient's experience.

One Friday morning as I was on my way to a presentation, I thought, *I'm certainly fortunate to be part of all these amazing interactions with patients. What a privilege to have a positive impact on people going through difficult circumstances.*

These thoughts grew and expanded. I hate to admit it, but they grew a bit beyond the bounds of healthy self-esteem. One might say they even grew to the point of self-aggrandizing, something like, "My, my, I'm certainly a fine fellow to be doing such wonderful work for such needy people."

Suddenly a small voice hijacked my ego trip and I heard: "You are the plastic bag!"

"What? I'm the plastic bag?"

"Yes, you are the plastic bag. The music is the medicine."

Ouch!

Anyone familiar with the infusion process knows that when patients arrive for treatment, they are checked in, interviewed by a nurse, and recent medical markers are reviewed. If everything is a "go," the order for the patient's medicine is sent to the lab. The lab formulates the chemo and places it in a plastic bag. The nurse hangs the plastic bag on an infusion pole, and a drip line connects the chemo to the patient. A flow meter is set up and the infusion process begins. When treatment is complete, the plastic bag and tubing are discarded.

OK, I get it. I'm the plastic bag, the container that carries the medicine. The music-medicine flows out, enhancing the healing process.

Thinking about the wisdom of the "small voice" has brought a great sense of relief. I'm just one little part of the healing process. In the same way doctors, nurses, and techs bring their knowledge and skills, I bring the gift of music. As a team, we work together for the best possible patient outcome. My part is to simply get filled up with music and transport it wherever it is needed. When my heart is full, I have something of value to give.

Of course, playing music is such an enjoyable endeavor that it's hard to convince anyone that I'm working. I must regularly explain that if a person is required to be at a certain place at a stated time and perform specific activities, that is work... no matter how much you enjoy it.

Here is my plastic-bag job description: Show up, bring your gifts and skills, put them into action, then stand back and watch your gifts become the medicine.

"I Never Promised You a Rose Garden"

– LYNN ANDERSON

I've had many jobs in my life: grass cutting, lawnmower repair, laying a sewer line, blowing up dynamite on a seismic crew, finish carpentry, pattern making, snow plowing, assistant thermometer operator, and coffee demo person (I only drink tea), to name a few. The appreciation for my labor at these jobs was expressed in the form of a paycheck, not words.

Playing music in a medical setting is completely different. Every day, I hear, "Thank you, I really appreciate what you're doing." "You don't know how much this music means to our family." Not only is there appreciation expressed by patients, I also hear it from my coworkers, doctors, nurses, medical staff, and housekeeping personnel. The affirmation comes in all sizes and shapes: head nods, thumbs up, fist bumps, handshakes, and pleasant conversation. Of course, by now you and I know that music is the medicine and I'm the plastic bag—but who doesn't appreciate being appreciated?

Lest you think playing music in a medical setting is a never-ending meeting of the mutual admiration society, let me expand the view.

"Move It On Over" (Hank Williams)

Early on in my hospital experience, I was playing quietly outside an open door on the cancer floor. A man abruptly popped out of the room and with some obvious irritation said, "Would you mind moving down the hallway? She's trying to sleep."

My goal is to comfort, not agitate, so I quickly moved down the hall.

When I saw the nurse manager, I let her know what had happened. She asked which room. When I told her, she thought for a moment, then said, "Sometimes when people are on this floor, they feel like their life is completely out of control. They will look for things that allow them to have a sense of control."

In the first decade of my hospital experience, that was the only negative interaction (mild as it was) I ever had with a patient or family member. Years later, I encountered something completely different.

"Have I Told You Lately That I Love You?" (Van Morrison)

I was playing in the lobby of the radiation area, taking requests from patients who had arrived early for their appointment. It was an old-school country sort of day; Johnny Cash, Willie Nelson, and Hank Williams were making toes tap.

Between songs, a gentleman walked in. I said, "Hi, how are you doing?"

I had carefully avoided this greeting in the early part of my career. It struck me as insensitive to ask anyone in the midst of cancer treatment how they were doing. After all, people don't come to the hospital expecting small talk and a cheerful concert. Sitting in the waiting area of a medical center isn't anyone's idea of a great day. "Hi" or "Good to see you" seemed a better choice.

However, I had paid attention to the way nurses and admins welcomed patients. What did they say as an appropriate greeting? Basically, "Good morning, Frank. How are you doing today?" The response was inevitably "Fine." After seeing and hearing this small ritual hundreds of times. I realized that a casual, "How ya doing?" is simply an act of acknowledgment. It's a recognition of our common humanity, shorthand for "I care about you."

Of course, with nurses "fine" isn't enough information. As soon as the patient is settled in, their attending nurse will take them through a detailed interview regarding their current medical status: Are you experiencing any pain? How is your appetite? Are you sleeping well? Are your bowels working properly? And much, much more.

After seeing this how-do-you-do verbal handshake operate in the same way as friends meeting on the street, I was comfortable with it... until this day.

This man's response was forceful and pointed. "How do you think I'm doing? I'm here to undergo a long and tortuous medical process that will be followed by injecting poisons into my body on the chance that one or the other of them might save me from a disease that is trying to kill me. My life has been completely overturned by this disease. I can't sleep, I can't work, and who knows if I'll even survive. How would you be doing?"

Yipes! So much for the pleasant acknowledgment of our common humanity!

Fortunately, I didn't need to respond. He turned immediately to Roberta, the admin, who checked him in. He then walked back through the glass entrance doors and stood in the hallway, phone in hand.

For the next eight weeks of his treatment, he followed the same routine: check in, stand out in the hall staring at his phone, waiting until he was called for treatment. On some days, if he made eye contact, I would say "Hi."

After four weeks, I asked Roberta if she had ever worked with another patient like this fellow. She smiled and said, "No, he's a tough one."

Fortunately, it's difficult for even the toughest individual to withstand compassionate concern. Roberta would get him checked in five days a week, and on days when I wasn't there, he would stay in the lobby, and they would talk.

She asked him why he stood outside the lobby on Tuesdays.

"I don't want the music to make me happy. I'm not happy going through this, and I don't want anyone trying to make me happy. I don't think anyone should be happy about having cancer."

On a different occasion, she asked about his support system. He told her he was a successful lawyer and had plenty of resources. Sadly, somewhere in the pursuit of that success, he had divorced a wife or two and had alienated his children.

Facing a difficult prognosis, he had asked Roberta, "What good is all that money if I don't live long enough to spend it?"

His story reminded me of the old Porter Wagoner hit "Satisfied Mind." *"But little they know that it's so hard to find, one rich man in ten with a satisfied mind."*

Obviously, I don't know this fellow's backstory, and it's not my business to understand how he came to this point in his life. Money and success can be very good things. I know many people who have parlayed their diligence and hard work into financial blessing for themselves, their family, and society at large. But there's another side to that coin. The love of money for its own sake can be a cruel and relentless taskmaster.

"Has Anybody Ever Told You" (Ashley Monroe)

One Tuesday afternoon, I was doing what I do, quietly playing relaxing music in an infusion area. This area was set up with a series of infusion bays along the window side of the room. Each bay had a privacy curtain on three sides. In front of the curtains was an aisle. Slowly coming toward me down the aisle was a woman pushing her walker. A relative was assisting with her chemo pole.

As she approached, I was definitely sensing a vibe.

Music is all about vibration, the vibe. As a matter of fact, the whole world is made up of tiny molecules constantly in motion. Everything has a vibe—a tree, a car, a sidewalk. They are all in motion on the molecular level.

For musicians, vibrations are the currency of our medium. Being "in tune" means that the sounds generated by an instrument are vibrating harmoniously together. When an instrument is out of tune it means that some of the vibrations being created are fighting against others. Fighting? Yes. We can't see it, but musical instruments create literal waves by moving molecules of air. When these back-and-forth motions align, the sound is harmonious. When they clash, *disharmony*.

People also have a vibe. It's great to meet a person who is on the same vibe, the same wavelength as you.

This concept goes to a higher level when we consider groups of people. For a musician, it's important to feel the vibe of a room. It's this sensing of energy, emotion, and attitude that gets us in tune with a crowd, be it on a hospital floor, a teenage dance, or a professional concert.

As I said, I was sensing a strong vibe from this woman, and it wasn't a groovy 70s vibe. She was approaching me with a scowl on her face, driving her walker like a bulldozer. And something about her vibe triggered the little voice in my head that said, "Don't react."

When she was within a foot of me, she stopped, looked me in the eye, and said, "Has anyone ever told you you're annoying?"

In my best neutral voice, I replied honestly. "No."

"Well, let me be the first," she snarled.

There was no need for any of the dozen responses that popped into my head.

She resumed her trek to the restroom.

I know that people experiencing cancer aren't feeling great and there are plenty of things in life that can make a person cross and bad-tempered, but 99.99 percent of my experiences with people in the hospital had been very positive. This was a real outlier. I knew that I hadn't done anything out of the ordinary that would give this lady cause for such a statement, but that doesn't mean it was easy to not be personally offended. I had a strong desire to respond in kind, but I've found it best to stick with the advice of that little voice, "Don't react."

As I was leaving for the day, I told one of the nurses what had happened, in case they received any negative feedback regarding that annoying guitarist. She immediately began to apologize and mentioned that the same patient had made nasty remarks about one of the other nurses, a nurse as sweet as sugar pie.

The next week when I returned, the nurse I had spoken with told me she had a conversation with our grumpy patient. It went something like this—

"Our patients really enjoy having live music here. John's not annoying; he's actually a nice guy."

Almost before the words were out of her mouth, the woman shot back, "No, he's not! He's not a nice guy! He's like all the other guitar players, just like my guitar-playing ex-husband!"

Yipes! Guilt by association. It's not my place to play amateur psychologist, but I think I was the target of some misplaced aggression. I'm sure this woman was wrestling with all kinds of medical and personal issues that had her behaving as less than her best self. I've sometimes accounted for this kind of reaction with what I call the "theory of the nearest target." If a person can't afford to blow up at their boss, they may release that anger on their spouse, their child, or even a random stranger—road rage!

One thing I try to keep front-of-mind: Everyone you meet is likely going through some difficulty in their life, and if we can train ourselves to extend grace in the face of hurtful words, the situation will de-escalate, and the world will be a better place.

I share this bit of advice with you, knowing that I am a work in progress.

"Tight Rope"

– LEON RUSSELL

Is it difficult to do what you do? This can be a tough question to answer.

For the first few years I played at the hospital, I had a recurring dream. In it, I received a cancer diagnosis. The dream began with a doctor breaking the news, followed by nurses explaining what to expect. I would wake up shaken, thinking I was sitting in an infusion chair, unsure if this was a dream or reality.

When working in a caring profession, it is easy to take on burdens that aren't our own. Being overly empathetic without having a way to process difficult emotions can be mentally and physically draining.

I've asked nurses how they deal with the inherent stress that comes with their work. Their answers boiled down to this: "We're trained professionals focusing on the patient, caring for each individual with empathy." That is exactly what I've observed over the years. But then comes the last tricky bit of advice: "When you go home, leave work at work." Easier said than done.

Sometimes I think of this stress as an internal rope. When I'm working, interacting with patients and their families, my rope is pulled tight. My attention is focused on bringing relaxation, comfort, and connection to the people I'm with. I am emotionally engaged, not emotionally overwhelmed. This tight rope of activity is wrapped around my heart and, in a sense, serves to hold me together. By actively entering the moment, I can fix my attention on what is, without worrying about what might be. But when I have an extended time away from work, a long weekend or a vacation, the rope slackens, allowing suppressed emotions to bubble to the surface suddenly and unexpectedly.

A few years ago, Connie and I planned a weeklong vacation. Day One was the Dublin Irish Festival, an annual event we always look forward to. For over 35 years, the city of Dublin, Ohio, has put on a world-class celebration of Irish music and culture. Central Ohio has a lively Celtic music scene, with plenty of top o' the heap musical talent. The icing on the cake is a boatload of the finest fiddlers, singers, and pipers straight from the Emerald Isle.

On this day, my inner rope was relaxed. It was my first significant time off in many months, a gorgeous, blue-sky Saturday. We were sitting beside the overflowing main stage tent, watching a group of Irish lads collectively known as Slide. Their performance was pure joy, the fiddle, the penny whistle, every instrument entwined in an ecstatic celebration of life. It was an overdose of delight. Unexpectedly, I was hit with an overpowering wave of sorrow—*Everyone in this tent, so joyful now, is headed for a hospital bed.* Though I knew this wasn't true, the thought captured me and the sadness ran deep. Pent up tears came like a flood, tears of joy mingled with tears of grief.

Early in my time at the hospital, I parked in the lot nearest the entrance used by folks going to the maternity floor. Every day I would see expectant parents walking in and wide-eyed parents rolling out with tiny baby bundles closely cradled. The hours between my comings and goings were spent with people struggling to stay alive. The distance from the door to the floor was a regular reminder of the beauty and brevity of life. This business of living is simultaneously amazing and heartbreaking, beautiful and broken.

Unwittingly, I had been framing my interactions with patients in cheerful optimism without recognizing the need for my own quiet contemplation. I needed time to reflect on their stories and ponder the things I had seen. While doing my best to pour out musical comfort to others, my own reservoir was running dry. No one can give away what they don't possess. I needed to allow the music to touch me in the same way it was impacting patients, families, and staff.

We all experience emotions that cannot be fully expressed in words. Music helps shape inexpressible feelings into something more tangible. That's why a movie soundtrack is so critical. It communicates what the director wants the viewer to feel without unnecessary dialogue.

In our daily lives, music can help us shape difficult emotions, hurts, and losses into something recognizable; it can help us resolve emotional loose ends. Music gives us permission to experience our feelings, good and bad.

Keeping the rope too tight for too long and repressing difficult memories is like trying to clamp down the lid of a boiling pot. Something is going to explode. Better to take off the lid, discuss, reflect, renew.

4

Unconventional Convention

"The Monster Mash"

– BOBBY PICKETT

"A lumberjack, a preacher, and a duck walk into a bar..." Lots of humor is based on imagining the improbable. It's an easy set up for comedians, but sometimes the improbable becomes the reality. Imagine this: A zombie, a cancer patient, and a role-playing gamer walk into a drum circle...

The Greater Columbus Convention Center was the venue for a major two-day cancer conference. There were general sessions, panel discussions, and workshops covering the latest research by top-notch cancer experts. Every presentation was focused on informing and educating. Topping it off was a keynote address by television personality and journalist Joan Lunden. In short, this was a big deal, high-profile event intended for anyone and everyone whose life had been touched by cancer.

Art therapist Jen and I were representing our department, Integrative Services. Jen set up an interactive art project. She taped fifteen-foot sheets of blank newsprint along the main corridor of the Convention Center. In front of this, she set up a table covered with a rainbow of art supplies, markers, pencils, brushes, and watercolor paints. All passersby were invited to express their inner artist. With my guitar strapped over my shoulder, I roamed the hall playing mellow instrumental music and engaging people in conversation.

There are some things that shouldn't be brought together.

Earlier, as I was making my way from the parking tower to our area of the convention center, I noticed a few people dressed in outlandish, highly detailed, and occasionally macabre Halloween costumes. Not entirely unexpected, as the convention center hosts all kinds of events.

When I arrived at my designated area, Donna, my contact for the convention, was checking people in. As she helped me get unpacked, she asked, "Did you hear what happened last night?" I had just arrived and hadn't seen or talked with anyone, beyond a "Hi" to a bloody pirate and a crazy clown.

Wide-eyed, she explained: "The Midwest Haunt Convention is taking place at the same time as the cancer conference. Can you imagine? A haunt convention!"

As an aside, did you know there is a professional American haunt industry? It's more than plastic skeletons and witch costumes. It's big bucks, as in over a billion dollars annually. Pretty scary indeed! Halloween is their peak season, but haunt events take place year-round. I had no idea about any of this until I helped a friend shoot a sci-fi haunt movie in exchange for a music video of me playing guitar in a dilapidated chicken coop... But I digress.

On the previous night, the haunt convention folks had parked a shiny black hearse in front of the main entrance of the convention center. This was the entrance through which most of the cancer patients and survivors would be arriving. To say the medical people were shocked and appalled would be an understatement. Of course, the haunt folks delight in all things shocking and appalling. They weren't happy about being asked to remove their visually provocative marketing prop. Negotiations were civil and quick. The hearse was removed.

What could not be removed was the sound.

The haunt conventioneers had taken up residence in one of the huge convention halls directly across from the cancer workshop area. The hallway between was "convention-center wide," but that wasn't wide enough! There were double doors that could be closed, but every time those doors opened, which was most of the time, a cacophony of groans, moans, screams, and bellows along with flashing lights, sirens, and general chaos came roaring out. Who or what was coming and going through those open doors? Axe murderers, zombies, blood-stained bandits, insane clowns, vampires, monsters named and unnamed. Yes, a perfect mix of anxiety-producing triggers.

There are some things that should be brought together.

While murder and mayhem were being promoted on one side of the hallway, the other side was dedicated to lifesaving research and education. Along with the scheduled cancer presentations, folks from the field of integrative medicine were asked to participate.

Integrative medicine is an interesting term. Originally, things like art therapy, music therapy, dietary consultation, massage, mind-body techniques, and acupuncture were grouped together as *alternative medicine.* That could sound needlessly antagonistic to a medical professional. Which alternative would you prefer? A doctor who spent countless hours studying and practicing the science related to the infinite variables of human health or someone who is offering what looks like a mixture of health food and hopeful wishes? If the clinical approach seems cold and impersonal, you may want to consider the weird, warm world of soft music and fragrant candles.

Fortunately, the medical community has realized that there is significant benefit in both approaches. Science focuses on bodily mechanics, while the alternatives deal with a patient's humanity. Wouldn't it be great to have a holistic blending of physics and metaphysics? Maybe both approaches could work together to touch everything that makes us human, not as combatants fighting one another but as companions working together on the same team, with the same goal. That's "integrative medicine," a much friendlier designation.

With this in mind, artists, musicians, and other soft science practitioners were invited to the conference. This would be an opportunity for integrative folks to demonstrate and discuss the benefits of their specialties. We were set up in classic trade show fashion with rows of tables and booths lining the hallways and surrounding meeting spaces. The change-over times between workshops and presentations was our opportunity to reach prospective clients.

Learning to play well with others

While cancer patients and survivors were in their workshops, I took the opportunity to meet the other integrative folks at their tables and booths. I moseyed over to a table covered with brochures, pictures, and a poster that read "Reiki." Two ladies, quiet and composed, were mindfully standing behind their display table. I introduced myself as "a guitarist," redundant perhaps, given the guitar slung over my shoulder.

"What do you ladies do?" Even though I was familiar with Reiki, it's usually best to let people describe their work in their own words.

Ladies: "We do energy work."

Me: "Like some kind of electrical charge?"

Ladies: "No, not like that. Are you familiar with acupuncture?"

Me: "Yes."

Ladies: "It's like that but without the needles."

Good angel on my right shoulder says: "Be nice, be civil."

Mischievous angel on my left says: "You'll never get a better setup than that."

The mischievous angel won.

Me (to the ladies): "Acupuncture without needles? Don't you think you're missing *the point*?"

The look was priceless. Without speaking a word, they communicated, *Get out of here. You're an idiot.*

Thank you, mischievous angel. It still makes me laugh.

Onward I wandered. A nurse from a related hospital had set up a drum circle with a dozen or so hand drums in a variety of sizes and shapes, all beautifully decorated with bright and cheery colors. She told me she conducted regular drum circles for patients and provided drums for individual patients to use during their stay in the hospital.

Everything was neat and orderly, a perfect circle of drums surrounded by a perfect circle of chairs. A lot of folks were milling around the hall. I asked if she would like to play some music together. Maybe we could attract a crowd for her circle.

"No, I'm not really a musician," she said. "I'll wait till some people sit down and then get something going."

This struck me as a little unusual. My approach is more like the movie *Field of Dreams:* "If you build it, they will come." Most people are very unlikely to initiate a musical experience without some level of invitation. At this event, we would be trying to corral people in motion. They would only pass through our area twice. Once on their way to a workshop and later, on their way to lunch.

As I turned to go, a local news reporter walked up to the circle. We had met years earlier when she interviewed me for a story on music and cancer. Her interest in cancer was both personal and professional. Several members of her family had been in the battle. We caught up for a few minutes, then she looked at the drums and said, "Do you want to play something together?"

I said, "Sure," and thought, *This should be interesting.*

In her dressed-for-TV clothes and makeup, the reporter looked more prepared to walk down a celebrity red carpet than to rock out on hand drums. Amazingly, she locked into a sophisticated smooth and steady jazz groove. I sprinkled in a few minor seventh chords, and we were able to gather a small crowd.

When we finished, she gave me a sly grin. "I was part of my high school drum line."

Looking at the crowd that had stopped to listen, it struck me that even though our target audience was cancer patients, there was another huge potential audience all around us—zombies, werewolves, and monsters. They could all benefit from learning about cancer prevention and treatment. Is there anyone who hasn't been impacted by cancer?

Jen, the art therapist, also realized this. She had been steadily recruiting, asking anyone who walked by to add words and pictures to her huge sheets of paper. This in-process masterpiece was eight feet high and fifteen feet long, plenty of room for abundant creativity. Across the top she had written, "What Cancer Can't Take Away."

Haunt and cancer people weren't the only ones convening on this Saturday morning. Down the north hallway in a large, quiet convention room, sat hundreds of folks, mostly guys. Rows of tables filled the room. It was eerily quiet, with scant conversation. Each person stared intently at the playing cards spread out in front of them. This was a tournament, a bloodless battle royale. These gamers were playing *Magic: The Gathering*, a fantasy and adventure card game.

One fellow had driven to Columbus from New Orleans for a shot at the $10,000 grand prize. He added a beautiful waterfall to the art in process. He then artistically hid the word "Spirit" inside of the river which Jen had drawn. As he was using the blue and green markers, he told me about a close friend and her battle with cancer, "a spirit who had gone over the waterfall too soon."

Haunters and gamers alike added to the picture while telling their cancer stories. These were moving, personal stories about their friends and families. Throughout the morning, this plain piece of paper turned into a vibrant memorial, a meaningful expression of "All the Things Cancer Can't Take Away." Prominent in this work were themes of faith, hope and love. Paper + colored markers + an invitation = Art.

Interestingly, all the monsters I spoke with were very human. I spotted a "killer clown" and had a picture taken with him. He easily engaged in a deep conversation about what was going on with the cancer convention. He was very appreciative of it. There were so many people in his life who had battled the disease.

While we were talking another haunter came over and introduced himself. He was getting ready to check into the hotel. Dressed in jeans and a t-shirt, he told me, "I'll be back shortly as a bloody maniac wrapped in chains. It makes a great Instagram shot." Turns out his organization does zombie events: mud runs, blood drives, zombie parades. Money from those events goes to charities: homeless shelters, food banks, and the like. Their tag line: "We play dead so others may live." Not the kind of benevolence one might expect from a bloody, shackled maniac.

So often we only see the trimmings and trappings. We miss what's on the inside. The handful of haunters I spent a few friendly minutes with looked like bloody, devil-worshiping crazies. The people I discovered inside the costumes were caring, compassionate individuals.

When the cancer attendees began to flow out of their first workshop, I hurried back to the drum circle. Three or four people had gathered. Instructions from the "I'm not a musician" musician, were simple:

"Follow me.

1 – 2 – 3 – 4,

bop, tap, tap, tap,

bop, tap, tap, tap."

Everyone was well behaved. Everything was proceeding slowly and peacefully, organized and controlled. A few more people sat down in empty chairs. More tapping.

bop, tap, tap, tap,

bop, tap, tap, tap

Suddenly, out of nowhere, there appeared a one-woman-hurricane with wild hair, flannel shirt, tattered jeans. I recognized this as the uniform of the haunt conventioneers. With a swoop of her arms, she gathered five drums to herself, crouched like a tiger guarding her cubs, and began playing all five drums at once, singing and shouting while giving instructions to the politely tapping drummers:

"Like this," she demonstrated.

BOOM, *tata, tata, tata, tata, tata, tata, tata.*

BOOM, *tata, tata, tata, tata, tata, tata, tata.*

The cadence quickened, syncopated staccato, polyrhythmic pounding, raucous rhythm, primal pulsing. People from every direction joined in. The circle grew.

This frenetic free-for-all continued to crescendo for about three and a half minutes. Suddenly another woman appeared, definitely not wearing the haunt uniform. She began talking loudly—no, shouting—trying to be heard over the rhythmic racket. It was a vain attempt to communicate with the dazed, supposedly in charge, "I'm not a musician" lady.

I didn't catch the entire conversation but what I heard was, "Stop this! Stop it! You must stop this now! We are conducting audiology tests upstairs, and we can't hear a thing!"

The wild woman who at this point was the ad hoc drummer in charge was totally oblivious to the conversation. She built the banging to a fevered pitch then signaled a dead stop by yelling, "That's it! **BOOM, BOOM, BOOM, BOOM. STOP!**"

Incredibly, the group followed her perfectly.

She jumped up from her ambush of drums (*ambush* the official name for a group of tigers) and exclaimed, "If you want CDs or more information, or if you want to do a haunted event, go to my website!" Like lightning, she passed out business cards to the entire drum circle, including spectators. Then she sprinted across the hall and disappeared into the chaos behind the double doors.

Doors closed. Peace descended. People proceeded to their next workshop.

During the second break, a drummer, or more accurately, a *capoeirista,* stopped by. Capoeira is a form of Brazilian martial arts accompanied by a drumbeat. I'm not sure which group he was with; best guess, he had been eliminated from the Magic tournament. He was not a wild haunter.

Slowly, he began playing two drums in a gentle bossa nova style. Several cancer patients joined. I added some guitar. Unlike the earlier sonic storm, this was the sound of a graceful dance, smooth and elegant. Not loud, but loud enough to attract the attention of the audiologist lady for a second time. The "not a musician" musician had vanished. The audiologist explained her problem again, this time to an authoritative-looking person who wasn't associated with the drumming. Fortunately, the authoritative person didn't need to respond. The Brazilian capoeirista had moved on.

Once again, peace prevailed. Everyone went to lunch.

I dropped in on the last general session of the day. Joan Lunden, master communicator that she is, told her very personal cancer story. She connected. With great empathy, she verbalized the struggles and fears of many in the room. Her battle with cancer was inspiring, informative, helpful, and hopeful.

What an amazing morning! What a convergence of people! The gift of music had once again immersed me in the ever-flowing river of life.

5

“Do You Come From a Land Down Under?”

— MEN AT WORK

"I've Got the Music in Me"

— THE KIKI DEE BAND

For centuries anthropologists, psychologists, musicologists, evolutionary biologists, and other "ologists" from all over the world have debated the origin and purpose of music. Opinions range from music is a worthless pursuit, a corrupter of youth that serves no evolutionary purpose, to music is a heavenly gift meant to expand our emotions, refine our intellect, and bless humanity. While I find music as mysterious and wonderful as many of these highly degreed thinkers do, I would like to offer a few thoughts based on my own experience.

First, I'm fully in the "heavenly gift" camp. As a creature made in God's image, I see music as something that originates in our humanity, a baked-in, core part of what it means to be human. If this unusual phenomenon which we call music appears in all known cultures (as it does), and if humans are created in God's image (as many folks believe), it seems reasonable to assume that music is a significant part of the divine nature.

So, what are the parts and pieces that make up music? A building is made of many distinctive elements: concrete, steel, wood, etc. Music is also composed of distinctive elements. Three of the most basic are: rhythm, melody, and harmony.

Rhythm. I know where you were, dear reader, the first time you experienced rhythm. It was the steady *pa-bomp, pa-bomp* of your mother's heartbeat combined with the regular in and out *whoosh* of her breathing. You were resting quietly, internalizing the rhythm of life.

Melody. Try speaking in a monotone for several minutes. When I present this concept to groups of young children, I switch to my staccato, emotionless "robot voice" and say, "If I were to speak to you like this for five minutes you would all fall asleep and miss all the good things I am going to say about melody." By the time I finish this silly sentence, the kids are laughing their heads off. Why? Because our normal speaking voices contain the rising and falling pitches that make even the tiniest spoken phrase melodic. This up-and-down sound heightens emotion, increases interest, and fine-tunes the meaning of our words. Even a young child can distinguish between a sarcastic "Right!" and the same word spoken in harmonious agreement.

Harmony. Speaking of harmony, examine the various weirdly shaped appendages that make up your body. If all these bodily pieces were a jigsaw puzzle, and you had never seen a human body, how would you put it all together? Maybe eyes on each side of the head? Ears at the front and back? What if your whole body consisted of just one large elbow or a giant foot? How would that work? Don't forget about all the weird and wiggly internal organs. How would you pack those into your skin suit? Our bodies are a collection of strange and oddly shaped parts that somehow work together to accomplish astounding things. This is an ever-present example of harmony built into our very being.

We could go on discussing other elements of music like dynamics, tempo, and timbre, but I think you get the point. All the elements of music are born out of our humanity.

Fortunately, we are not limited to the sounds our bodies can make. Human creativity has devised musical instruments that allow us to make sounds that are higher, lower, and more harmonic than anything we could accomplish with our bodies alone.

Of course, the business of making sound is not the same as making music. Sound occurs anytime something vibrates. It could be the sound of a pencil tapping on a desk or a jackhammer breaking up concrete. Sounds are not music until they are organized into some sort of meaningful form. The sound of an orchestra tuning up isn't music. The downbeat of the conductor's baton transforms random musical sounds into rhythm, melody, and harmony, into the mysterious art of authentic music.

Can sound have meaning? This is easily answered when talking about language. Every word that has ever been spoken is made of sounds that have been assigned meaning. These word sounds are capable of naming things that we can touch and see and of conveying the meaning of abstract concepts like truth and freedom.

Musical sounds convey meaning too. While instrumental music doesn't communicate in a practical, literal sense—"Which way to the restroom?" or "Time to take out the trash"—it does communicate in a manner that significantly engages the listener emotionally and intellectually.

No wonder music is called the universal language. It reaches across cultures by communicating emotion with or without words. Music can produce feelings that enhance and transcend spoken language because it is born out of our common humanity. These sonic vibrations we call music speak from one heart to another.

This helps to explain why music, vocal and instrumental, is so effective in healing situations. Offbeat internal rhythms can sync up to external rhythmic patterns. Out-of-tune thoughts and feelings can be brought into harmony and redirected in a positive direction. Good vibes can smooth out our internal rhythms. Just as a steady beat can align the actions of groups of people—soldiers marching or dancers dancing—it can also bring chaos, internal or external, into order. It can move what is unwell toward a place of healing.

"Walk Like an Egyptian"

– THE BANGLES

I was standing near the bank of elevators when the nurse manager rushed over, gripped my elbow insistently, and said, "Come with me."

As we hurried down the hall, she quickly explained. "An Egyptian woman was just transported to this floor. She is extremely agitated. She doesn't speak any English, and her family isn't here yet." When we arrived at the patient's door, her parting words were, "Go in there and do what you do."

When I entered the room, a woman was lying on top of the bed. She was wearing a head scarf that revealed only her face. Her plain dress came down to her ankles. To say she was distraught doesn't begin to describe the scene. Her arms were flailing, her feet were up in the air kicking, she was crying and calling out in a language I had never heard. She looked like a person who was trying to run, swim, and drown all at the same time. I didn't think "Take Me Home, Country Roads" was going to work in this situation!

A few months prior to this, I met a Chinese interpreter. This was before online translators replaced in-person interpreters. He and I had a delightful conversation regarding culture, communication, and cuisine. His work had provided him with plenty of challenging and unusual situations. Ah-ha, here was a person who might provide some firsthand insight into a question I had been pondering.

"I play music for lots of people, some of whom are from China and don't speak English. I don't know any Chinese songs. I don't even understand that system of music. When I have the opportunity to play music for someone from China, what should I do?" I asked.

"No problem," he said. "It's actually very easy. Just play 'Twinkle, Twinkle, Little Star.' Everyone in China knows that song."

In my mind, I was thinking, *What! There are over a billion people in China, and you're telling me they all know 'Twinkle, Twinkle, Little Star'?*

"OK, if you say so."

Back in the hospital room, as I looked at a lady who wasn't Chinese, I was hoping that lovely lullaby had made its way to Egypt.

I began playing a relaxing instrumental version of this cradlesong, then added the lyrics. These words are so familiar that we may not recognize them as the night-sky celebration they truly are. "*Up above the world so high, like a diamond in the sky.*"

Sure enough, after a couple of verses, the flailing, kicking, and crying slowed, then stopped. She settled into the bed. After doing all the twinkling that seemed appropriate, I moved into a time of calm improvisation in the same lullaby style and continued at a soothing tempo.

Twenty minutes later, several young adults in their late teens and early twenties arrived. They began hugging and comforting their beloved mom. The six-string Nightingale and I faded from this starlight reunion into the unrelenting noontime of the fluorescent hallway.

This is one reason why I am convinced that music is the universal language. A childlike melody brought relief to a stranger in a strange land. No intelligible words were exchanged. My observation: "Twinkle, Twinkle, Little Star" is a significant part of the musical *lingua franca*.

"How Sweet the Sound"

– CITIZEN WAY

It was Tuesday afternoon, and I had just arrived in the infusion area. In the bay to my far right, a young woman lay in bed, receiving chemo. Huddled together beside the bed were three women with long, straight black hair. One additional woman in the room didn't appear to be part of this group. She was seated beside the privacy curtain that had not yet been drawn. I heard quiet conversation between the three but didn't recognize the language. The lady sitting apart from the others walked over and introduced herself to me as Jia Li, a Chinese interpreter.

"Do you know 'Amazing Grace'?" she asked.

"Sure."

"In Chinese?

"Uuuhh...is the melody the same?"

"Come with me."

We joined the group alongside the bed and exchanged greetings. Two of the ladies beside the bed were sisters of the patient. The third lady was their mother.

Jia Li pulled out her phone and said, “OK, follow this.” It was a Chinese lyric video of “Amazing Grace.” She hit the “play” arrow, and the Chinese characters began to scroll slowly across the screen. Thankfully, it was the familiar melody. Jia Li sang and I accompanied, playing just loudly enough to cover the sound coming from the phone.

It worked; we made it through the song! I was thinking, *Look at me, I'm playing Chinese worship music! What a breakthrough in international relations!*

But that was only the beginning.

“That was good,” Jia Li said. “Now let's do this.”

She pulled up another lyric video. This time, it wasn't a well-known hymn. It was something I'd never heard before. Providentially, it sounded like a contemporary American worship song—basic chords and melody, not too difficult to figure out on the fly. Jia Lia had a quick exchange with the women. All I understood was heads nodding “yes.” We followed up with another similar song.

I was on a roll, now thinking, *Hooray, I've just played two Chinese songs that I've never heard before. Quick, somebody call the Nobel committee. Surely there is a Peace prize somewhere in all of this.*

But wait. Jia Li looked at me. “Very nice. Now let's do this one.”

Uh oh, we were heading to the deep end of the pool! It was a contemporary Chinese worship song but not in the style of any western music. Lyrics, rhythm, melody, chord progression, all unfamiliar. Thankfully, with Jia Li's lovely singing and a restrained approach to my playing, we made it through without any song-stopping missteps.

During this whole time, the women by the bed sat quietly smiling, sometimes with eyes closed, other times with encouraging looks toward each other.

I wish I had known the background of these ladies. I'm sure there was plenty to tell. What brought them to America? How were things going as they were learning to acclimate to this strange new culture?

Except for Jia Li, none of the women were conversant in English beyond a tentative "hello" and "thank you." Despite my limited understanding of the Chinese language and culture, this was a beautiful experience of music bridging the cultural gap. We were able to create an atmosphere that was meaningful and comforting. Words that no one else in the infusion area understood joined with melody to bring a touch of the familiar to an unfamiliar setting. It was a musical hug to the hearts of a patient, her mother, and her sisters.

– STING

It was a Wednesday morning, and I was in an infusion center. On this day, I noticed a young man in his mid-30s peeking around the privacy curtain of an infusion bay. He seemed very curious about the music.

I stepped over to the infusion bay and saw him sitting beside a slightly older fellow who was attached to a chemo line. They both had big smiles, curly dark hair, and cappuccino-colored skin. It quickly became apparent that English wasn't their first language. I didn't recognize the sound of their words. It wasn't Spanish or Portuguese. Maybe Arabic? My repertoire of Arabic songs was zero!

Hmmm, I'm a little uncertain where this might be going musically.

Doing this kind of in-the-moment work is at times like improv comedy. From what I know of improv, the key is being willing to say, "Yes, and...," then improvise the next section of the story. In other words, acknowledge the reality of the situation or comic setup, no matter how bizarre, and go with it.

OK, I'm stepping in.

"Any kind of music you would like to hear?"

Through hand motions and broken English, I learned that the patient was a singer and multi-instrumentalist. His friend was a percussionist. After a bit more of this mixed-media conversation, the friend said, "Sting!"

Yay! One of my favorite musicians. I know a bunch of Sting's music. This will be easy.

I began playing a graceful fingerstyle arrangement of "Every Breath You Take."

Before I was through the intro, in an accent that I still couldn't quite discern, the friend briskly said, "No, no, not that one, *chebmamie, chebmamie*!" I had no idea what he was saying.

"Uhhh, what's that again?"

"Cheb Mami, Cheb Mami, Rose, Desert Rose."

I was still not linking up with what was being communicated. He continued excitedly, "Cheb, sing with Sting, Algerian. So are we!"

Ahh, then I was on board. Later, I did some research and found out that Cheb Mami is a famous Algerian raï (Algerian folk music) singer and songwriter. He received worldwide attention when he added his amazing vocals, singing in Arabic to Sting's song "Desert Rose."

OK, got it.

I began explaining that I loved the song but didn't know it well enough to do it justice. I asked if there was something else they would like to hear.

I could see the nuances of my explanation were not connecting. As I've said, English wasn't the main mode of communication here. Maybe when I said, "don't know how to play it," all they heard was "play it"!

Whatever the case, the fellow in the chair started singing in Arabic and his friend began beating his chair like a hand drum. *OK, just say, "Yes and..." go with it!* I found a C minor chord, four beats, then Bb, I think. Yes, we were off and running.

They sang in Arabic, then I joined with dreams of rain and gardens.

It was far from a perfect rendition, but it was a great experience of music crossing cultural borders and bringing joy to two young men a long way from home.

Simply say, "Yes, and..." Take the world as you find it. Add something positive and enjoy the ride.

"Jammin'"

– BOB MARLEY

One Wednesday afternoon, I stepped into the patient lounge on the cancer floor to join Jean for the weekly High Tea. Jean is a retired music teacher and church organist with an encyclopedic knowledge of many styles of music. She has accompanied singers and choirs of all ages for over thirty years. She was just finishing Frank Sinatra's version of "New York, New York." I joined her for the next tune, which was from another up-tempo Broadway musical.

As we were playing, three Black women and a young girl seated in front of us were quietly talking together. I picked up a bit of a Jamaican accent in their whispered conversation. It wasn't too much of a stretch, given the Rastafarian colors and clothing they were wearing.

As Jean and I were on our musical stroll down Broadway, I detected a little eye-rolling from the ladies as they looked in our direction. If my perception was correct, I was sensing, "Well, that tune is very noisy and very white."

When we finished the song, one of them said, "How about a little Marley?" I'm pretty sure she was expecting a response along the lines of, "What's a Marley?"

Instead, I said, "Sure."

Leaning over to Jean, I said, "Key of C, walk down, follow my lead, plenty of syncopation, don't hit anything on the downbeat."

We launched into "No Woman, No Cry." The women in front of us grew quiet, listening. We finished the song, then another quick whisper to Jean: "Key of A, same syncopation." We continued jammin' on "Three Little Birds," one of Bob Marley's joyful songs of hope and comfort.

When we finished, the lady who had asked for some Marley was drying her eyes. "Thank you, that was just what I needed. You don't know how much it means to me. We're going through a lot right now with my mother being here."

One of the most significant gifts music offers is its ability to connect and comfort. Regardless of background or cultural heritage, the language of the heart builds bridges.

Dealing with cancer is never easy but the right song at the right time can work its magic. There is an assurance that all of us walking through this thing we call "life" are figuring it out together. As Marley's song says, as we push on through, "every little thing" and every big thing "is gonna be alright."

"The Sound of Music"

– RICHARD RODGERS AND OSCAR HAMMERSTEIN II

When I entered the room, an elderly woman lay in the bed. On the couch were two younger women who appeared to be daughters and a fellow on a nearby chair, perhaps a son-in-law. When I asked if they would like to hear some music, the daughter sitting closest to the young man (who I took to be her husband) immediately spoke up.

"Who wouldn't want to hear some music?" she said. "Music helps everything!"

I detected a hint of some African dialect in her voice, so I began playing a lively instrumental tune that I hoped sounded African. After a few seconds, she asked if I knew "Amazing Grace." I quickly realized that the music I was attempting probably sounded about as authentic as a cowboy singing opera.

She joined in on the first verse of "Amazing Grace" and continued till the end. Her voice had a rich, silky quality. Her sister smiled and quietly observed.

When we finished, the singing sister told me how much she enjoyed that song. She had learned it in English by listening to an international radio program that played a lot of hymns. I asked her if she would like to hear "How Great Thou Art."

"Yes, please."

As I began to play, she started singing, but I didn't recognize the words. She leaned over to her husband and said, "I only know this one in Swahili."

I had only heard Swahili in bits and pieces before and, of course, had never sung in that language. I asked if she would like to sing the song solo.

"No," she demurred. "You go ahead and sing. I'll just sing along."

We continued with our bilingual duet. The fluidity of her voice brought the familiar melody to life, even with unfamiliar lyrics.

The sound and phrasing of words varies from language to language. Some languages are harsh and clipped, others smooth and flowing. The sound of a language naturally influences the culture's vocal arts, its singing, speaking, and poetry. Italian, the *bella lingua* (beautiful language), certainly played a part in forming the sound of Italian Opera.

Once when I was on a musical mission to Sweden and Denmark, a Swede pulled me aside and said, "Danes sing like they have mush in their mouths. I can't understand a thing they are saying." An interesting comment, considering that both languages have similar vocabularies. I'm not taking sides, but there is a difference in how they pronounce their words, and it carries through in their singing too. On another occasion, I was part of a musical program featuring a historical reenactor who played the part of Jenny Lind. The original Jenny Lind was a Swedish opera singer who won the hearts of Americans in the 1800s under the sobriquet "the Swedish Nightingale." Did her native language influence her singing and success? I'm no linguist, but I'm guessing, yes.

I'm also no expert on African languages, but I will say, Swahili worked wonderfully well for this classic hymn. Best of all, the singing spoke deeply to the matriarch resting in the bed. As she received treatment with her family near, the sound of her daughter brought a smile and a tear.

Music, the language from the head to the heart,
Music, the language we've known from the start.
JDM

"The Condor Flies By" ("El Condor Pasa")

– PERUVIAN FOLK SONG

When I arrived at the infusion center, one of the nurses came to me immediately with a sheepish grin on her face. "I may have stepped in the poop this time."

This curly-haired nurse with big glasses was a huge music fan. When I played anything from the Woodstock era, she would send a smile, a wave, and a thumbs up. Her explanation: "I was raised by a hippie mom. She loved all that music, and so do I."

Most days, she would greet me with, "The person in #4 (infusion bay) likes country music," or "You've got a rock fan in #7." She was one of my informal booking agents. She would always tell patients, "The guitar guy is coming today; he takes requests."

"So," I asked, "what does, 'stepping in the poop this time' mean?"

"OK, here's the deal. Do you know any Peruvian folk songs? The lady in #6 would like to hear a Peruvian folk song."

Yipes, that's not a request I get every day! My mind began to spin.

Fortunately, a few days earlier, a gentleman had requested "El Condor Pasa," a song which Simon and Garfunkel recorded on their *Bridge Over Troubled Water* album. I knew it was from somewhere in South America, but what country? A quick Google search and, sure enough, it's from Peru. In 2004, the Peruvian government had it declared part of their national cultural heritage.

My hippie nurse/booking agent told me the lady who made the request was going to be receiving her first chemo treatment in a few minutes and was feeling very anxious about what might be in store. "I have a couple more things to do to prep her, then I'll invite you over."

When I came into the infusion bay, the woman was sitting quietly by herself. After a quick hello, she removed her sunglasses. I told her I only knew one Peruvian folk song. She said that was fine, anything would be great. I began "El Condor Pasa" instrumentally. She watched my fingers intently. As I began to sing, her eyes got misty. The lyrics began to flow; so did her tears.

When I finished, she told me that as a teenager in Peru she had regularly played guitar with friends. "'El Condor Pasa' was one we played every time. It was exactly what I was hoping to hear today." She had been in the States for over 20 years and had experienced much professional success as a writer. The music brought back pleasant memories of her adolescence and her friends. She described hearing this treasured melody as the first whiff of a long-forgotten treat, like warm, homemade sweet bread fresh from the oven. The music brought back a fragrance that woke the bittersweet memory of home and a happy childhood.

When the nurse returned with the plastic bag of chemo, my Peruvian friend was settled and ready to begin her new journey.

6

“Softly As I Leave You”

— ELVIS PRESLEY

"I'll Fly Away"

– ALBERT BRUMLEY

It was the Wednesday before Thanksgiving and I was playing lively acoustic music (Crosby, Stills & Nash and other 70s singer-songwriters) for a Vietnam veteran. Midway through our time together, I heard a heartrending wail from across the hall. I continued to focus on the patient at hand, but the cry echoing down the corridor was troubling.

My time with the vet had been very encouraging; his treatment was working, and he was on the mend. This visit was very upbeat with lighthearted laughter and joking. When we finished our time together, I stepped into the hallway, unsure of what I would find. Waiting outside the door was a young woman, eyes red from crying.

"Would you play for my brother?" She paused. "He just died. He really loved guitar music."

"Sure."

When we entered the room, Mom and Dad were sitting side by side on the couch. Mom's sobbing was unrestrained; she had lost her firstborn. Dad had a stoic expression and tear-stained eyes. In the bed was a young man who appeared to be in his early thirties. Both arms were colorfully tattooed sleeves. His hair was neatly slicked back. If someone had told me that he had just stepped off his Harley, walked into this room, and fallen asleep, I would have believed them. There were no outward signs of any illness.

Dad spoke. "Our son really liked bluegrass music."

I began with an instrumental version of "May the Circle Be Unbroken." The verses have to do with the loss of a mother, so I only sang the chorus. "*There's a better home a-waiting in the sky, Lord, in the sky.*"

Dad followed up with a specific request. "Can you play 'I'll Fly Away'?"

This time, the lyrics were right on target. *"Some bright morning when this life is over, I'll fly away..."* Dad and daughter sang harmonies. Mom cried quietly.

Was this fellow the favored son or the family rebel? I can't say. All I know is that he was loved, and he was gone.

The crossing from life to death is like the flipping of a switch, an irreversible switch.

"No more cold iron shackles on my feet, I'll fly away, I'll fly away..."

Death, like cancer, does not discriminate. Rich, poor, young, old, beautiful, plain, wise or otherwise, we all come with an expiration date. Most of the people I play for will fight through to another day. Many folks will return to their normal lives and experience remission. Still, when working with people battling a deadly disease, it's not surprising to come face to face with the reality of our mortality.

"Remember When"

– ALAN JACKSON

It was September 11, 2022. The news feed was abuzz on this twenty-first anniversary of the attack on the World Trade Center.

I was playing music in the north hallway when a woman in her early 70s carrying a bag of food from the cafeteria invited me into a room. As I entered, she introduced me to her daughter, who was sitting quietly in a chair on the far side of the bed. Sitting up in the bed, but unresponsive, was a middle-aged man with shaggy gray hair that joined his salt and pepper beard.

"Can you play something for my son-in-law?" the woman asked. "He likes anything country."

His wife looked up. "Do you know 'Folsom Prison Blues'?"

When I finished the song, the mother pointed. "Look at that! This is the longest he's kept his eyes open all day."

Yes, his eyes were open, but not in a good way. They were wide open, unblinking, staring blankly toward some place far beyond the wall in front of him. He hadn't made a sound since I arrived.

The wife asked for "Remember When" by Alan Jackson. I knew that Alan Jackson had memorialized the 911 attack in a song and thought she might have had a reason for reflecting on this historic event.

Both ladies were nervously talking to me at the same time while I searched through my tablet. With the competing conversations vying for my attention, it took longer than usual to find the right song file.

"If you can't find that one, just play anything country," said the mother.

But I could tell the wife had a personal reason for the song she requested. Just as I clicked on "Remember When," she said, "I've already made his picture video with this song as the soundtrack."

A younger me wouldn't have recognized the significance of that comment. In this setting, I knew exactly what it meant—an impending memorial service.

As the lyrics popped up on the screen, I remembered that Alan Jackson's 911 song was, "Where Were You (Went the World Stopped Turning)." The requested song was something completely different. "Remember When" is a tender recounting of a tough marriage with plenty of heartache. It's a chronological overview beginning when "I was young and so were you," and it follows the couple till "we turned gray." In the middle, "We came together, fell apart, and broke each other's hearts."

Reflecting on a lifetime of marriage can be emotionally charged in any setting. On this day, with end-of-life literally staring us in the face, it took everything I could do to keep from breaking down. When I glanced at the wife, her face was buried in her hands. Her shoulders were shaking.

Somehow, we made it through the song, but when I finished, she was still weeping, unable to look up. Between heart-rending sobs, she said, "Thank you. You'll never know how much that meant to me."

She was exactly right. I never know when a song will speak straight to a person's heart and circumstances. Often, there are feelings and memories buried deep within that need to be expressed. That mysterious combination of melody, harmony, and lyric reaches into places that nothing else can touch. Then tears will wash us on the inside.

Stepping back into the hallway, I was visibly shaken. The nurse attending this patient was walking toward me. She stopped, gave me an understanding look. "Are you OK?" A quick hug, then she entered the room. It took several minutes to compose myself, then onward, down the hall.

"Time"

– PINK FLOYD

Being a creature of habit, I have a series of hallway locations that I cycle through during my three-hour visits to the cancer floor.

It was a Monday afternoon in October. I had been on the floor for about forty-five minutes and was playing at my third location. A middle-aged man approached and asked if I could stop by his father-in-law's room and play some music. The room was at the end my regular circuit, and normally I would arrive in that area in about an hour and fifteen minutes.

I asked if there was any hurry. He said, "No whenever you have time."

Previous experience had taught me that "now" is usually the best time to respond to this type of request. In a busy medical environment with pending procedures, doctor visits, and the fickle nature of sleep and rest, it's important to provide a meaningful musical experience when the opportunity presents itself. I finished the song I was playing and headed to the room.

The father-in-law was in the bed, unresponsive. The gentleman who invited me was there with his wife. There were also several grown children. When I asked what kind of music her father would enjoy, the daughter replied, "Anything. He likes all kinds of music and hymns."

"In the Garden" seemed like a good starting place. The daughter smiled and said, "That was Mom's favorite." I also played "Amazing Grace." The daughter joined in and sang. We had a brief conversation, and they thanked me for coming. I resumed my normal circuit.

About ten minutes later, the couple came around the corner. She was red-eyed. He had a comforting arm around her shoulder.

"Father just passed," she said. "Thank you for playing. I think that's exactly how he would have wanted it."

Lesson for the day: "Now" is the best time—and sometimes the only time—to do what should be done.

"Chapel of Love"

– THE DIXIE CUPS

After lunch on a Monday, I walked into the nurse's breakroom where Chaplain Steve was sitting at a table, writing diligently in his notebook. As I was unpacking my guitar, he greeted me and asked, "Have you ever played for a wedding?"

I could have said I've played for weddings in houses, forests, and fields. I've played for weddings beside swimming pools and inside country clubs. I've been surrounded by stained glass while standing on stained carpet. I've accompanied flautists, flutists, violinists, pianists, singing cousins, and kilted bagpipers. I've played as the bride and her father arrived in a fairy-tale, gold-trimmed carriage pulled by a snow-white stallion while tiny spiders floated out of the forest canopy and landed on my fretboard. I've played for weddings where circling cicadas used the top of my head as a landing strip. I've played "Jesu, Joy of Man's Desiring" for fifteen minutes straight while the wedding coordinator frantically signaled "Keep going!" (The bride's grandmother hadn't found her way to the church yet.) I've played for in-laws, outlaws, and people wearing overalls, but the short answer to this question was, "Yes."

"Good. Meet me in room 23 at 2:30."

The reason Chaplain Steve popped the question became clear as I made my rounds. The doctor had informed his patient, "If there is anything in life you've been waiting to do, now is the time to do it."

The woman on the receiving end of this message had one big item on her bucket list. She and the man in her life had been together for twenty-three years but they hadn't gotten around to officially tying the knot. Today would be the day. This decision sparked a flurry of activities. One social worker went shopping for a dress, another set off in search of a wedding cake.

In the meantime, I was mentally reviewing appropriate wedding music for this occasion. Based on the age of the couple, one song quickly came to mind, "The Wedding Song" by Paul Stookey, of Peter, Paul and Mary fame. During the 70s and 80s, there must have been an unwritten law requiring the performance of this song before any marriage could be considered legitimate.

When I arrived, the family was gathered. The bride was lying in bed, wearing an elegant, light blue chiffon dress. The groom was slightly casual in his dark sport coat and tie. The two older sons must have come straight from the woods when they received the call. They were clad in camo cargo pants with matching camo caps. Thankfully, it isn't clothing that makes a wedding, it's the knitting of hearts—and that was on display in abundance. This small gathering was a tender acknowledgement of a loving, long-term relationship. The groom kissed the bride, the cake was cut, and peaceful music filled the room.

As mentioned, I've been part of many weddings. The first contact often comes by text, phone, or email. It's probably the result of a word-of-mouth referral, a Google search, or occasionally a hospital connection.

One very memorable wedding took place at a small private campground in rural central Ohio. My first contact for this wedding was an out-of-the-blue conference call. The couple was simply looking for fun love songs and a little instrumental music for the sand ceremony. The songs were no problem, but I had to look online to find out what a sand ceremony was.

When I arrived, everything was as expected, a beautiful cabin surrounded by tall maple trees and outlying campsites. When I met the officiant, the bride's brother, things began to get strange. There was something odd about his wedding garb. He was wearing a tuxedo with tails, which stood in sharp contrast to his black and white Chuck Taylor high-top tennis shoes. As friends and family began to arrive, the array of clothing grew increasingly weird. There were fashionable party dresses alongside Hawaiian shirts. Women in Kentucky Derby hats mingling with men in Bermuda shorts. There was everything from stylish and stately to mixed and motley, but one fashion statement tied it all together: the plentiful pairs of black and white Chucks.

After the half-hour musical prelude, the bride's younger brother accompanied her down the aisle. Then her older brother began the service. There were the expected greetings and wedding prayers followed by a little more music while the bride and groom poured different colors of sand into a single vase. This sand ceremony, new to me, was a beautiful metaphor for the blending of their lives. Then came a solemn moment recognizing parents, present and deceased. This thoughtful acknowledgment was followed by completely unexpected vows.

The bride's older brother turned to the groom and asked, "Do you solemnly promise to always close the toilet seat?" Then to his sister, "From this day forward, do you promise to always put the cap on the toothpaste?" Then to both, "Do you promise to surrender the TV remote whenever your spouse requests it? Do you promise to make milkshakes for one another without advance notice? Do you promise never to put cold feet on your spouse's back in the middle of the night?" And on it went. Friends and family were laughing and cheering.

The service ended with, "Now, by the power vested in me by no one in particular, I and this rowdy crowd declare you man and wife. You may kiss the bride!" More laughter and applause! I've seen a lot of unusual things during weddings, but never anything like this.

As I was packing up my gear, the jovial officiant walked over. "Dude," I said, "this was the craziest wedding I have ever been part of."

He laughed. "This wasn't their real wedding. They've been married for over two years. Back then, our dad was very sick. He heard you playing in the hospital and got your business card. When they realized there wasn't much time left, they had their official wedding in the hospital with a real pastor and immediate family. Before he passed, Dad gave them your card, looking forward to today. He wanted them to have a real celebration when they were ready for it."

In my mind, this gathering instantly transformed from the craziest wedding of all time to an awe-inspiring expression of selfless love. The bride's father, nearing the end of his life, was planning for his daughter's future happiness. He understood that weeping may last for a night, but joy comes in the morning, even if that morning is more than two years away. He knew the night would pass and there would again be joy and celebration for his family.

After the dark times
full of despair,
the sun slowly rises and
joy will be there.
- JDM

What was going on with the Chucks? I never found out, but intuition tells me their dad's gift of humor was one more treasure handed down.

– PAUL SIMON

Many of my musical adventures begin like this: A middle-aged woman is walking toward the elevators. She stops, listens, and asks: "Can you play for my mother? She loves music."

That is exactly what happened this day.

The woman took me to the room where her mother was sitting upright in the bed, looking very prim and proper. Her father was sitting quietly on the couch, late afternoon sunlight peeking over his shoulder through drawn curtains. There was a brief introduction by the daughter: “Look what I found in the hallway!” Then she disappeared.

During our small talk, I noticed this lady had the mannerisms of Katharine Hepburn. Something in her deportment conveyed a sense of dignified sophistication, independence and a strong will befitting a queen of the silver screen. The conversation moved to music, and I asked, “What kind of music do you enjoy?”

“What do you know?”

Judging her to be in her mid to upper 70s, I suggested Frank Sinatra.

“That would be fine.”

I played “The Way you Look Tonight” and “Fly Me to the Moon.” She appeared to enjoy those tunes but as soon as I finished, she asked, “What else do you know? Anything by Paul Simon?”

Oh yes, Paul Simon! I was ready. I had my tablet and plenty of his songs worked up. “Do you have a favorite song?”

I was expecting a request for something from the early Simon and Garfunkel catalog, perhaps “Homeward Bound,” “The Sound of Silence,” or “I Am a Rock,” something folky and intellectual. I was mildly shocked and pleasantly surprised when she said, “Do you know ‘Graceland’? I enjoy that very much.”

“Graceland.” Not what I would have expected from a person of this age but hey, no problem. Oh, if I could only have a backup band like Ladysmith Black Mambazo for a time like this! But we work with what we have, six strings and a melody.

Paul's lyrics begin with a shining picture of the Mississippi delta. Such an amazing song on so many levels.

When I finished, she said, "You know, I saw Paul in concert twice on his Graceland Tour. It was marvelous." She continued to tell me how much she enjoyed "Earth, Wind and Fire" several other jazz-pop bands and, of course, the Beatles.

Lesson for the day: Age doesn't necessarily determine a person's musical taste.

Several days later I received a phone call from her daughter. "Mother is out of the hospital now. She and Father would like you to stop by the house and play some music for her." Interesting. I hadn't done house calls for hospital patients before, but "yes" is often the best way to learn about life. I had to smile when she asked me, "Are you familiar with Worthington Hills?"

Worthington Hills is a very nice golf-course neighborhood just north of the Columbus outer belt. A few years earlier, I had been the nomadic guitar teacher in this neighborhood for years. It was when Taylor Swift was breaking onto the music scene. I taught many young girls "Tears on My Guitar" and many young boys Guitar Hero riffs.

When I made my house call, the husband greeted me at the door and politely thanked me for coming. He took me to the living room, where his wife was seated. The house was tastefully decorated and finely furnished in a style straight out of 1972 *Better Homes and Gardens*. She was sitting in a comfortable but straight-backed chair, and the expression on her face was somewhat strained, an expression I have seen when people battling cancer try to hide the pain and discomfort they are experiencing. Isn't it amazing to realize that "feeling normal" is actually an unappreciated state of bliss?

As the music began, she relaxed. Her husband brought me a glass of ice water in a cut glass tumbler, the fancy kind my mom would break out when we had special guests. We started with the Beatles, followed by "Frankie" (there was only one "Frankie" for this fan—Frank Sinatra). That led to some jazz-pop.

Then with a funny look on her face, she said, "This may sound strange, but do you know anything by Shirley Temple? When I was a little girl, my folks used to stand me on the grand piano and have me sing Shirley Temple songs."

My musical database contains many unusual and unexpected songs that have been requested over the years. Yes, I had worked up a song sheet for "Baby Face." I pulled it up on my tablet and gave it a spin. It brought a smile.

After about a half hour, she asked for "Graceland," and she again told me how much she had enjoyed seeing Paul Simon on the Graceland tour.

Her husband escorted me to my car. He asked, "Could you come back next week? This really helps her."

The following week when her husband met me at the door, he said, "She's not feeling too well today." She was sitting in the den in a more comfortable chair than the previous week but again with a strained countenance. We went through our familiar set list with James Taylor substituting for Frank Sinatra. About halfway through, she said, "We have some things we would like to give you, nice things, but things the children don't want."

I've noticed this on several occasions. As a person realizes they are nearing the end of their life, they want to give away things that are meaningful to them, something to be remembered by.

Then she looked me in the eye and said, "Do you know that Graceland is heaven? When Paul sings about Graceland, he is singing about heaven. I'm going there very soon. Would you play that song for me?"

Have I mentioned that singing through tears is part of the job description for this kind of work?

When her husband escorted me to the car this time, it was by way of the garage. There were three boxes packed up. Two with very nice Christmas ornaments and a box of cassette tapes and CDs: Earth, Wind and Fire, Beatles, some jazz, Frank Sinatra, and, of course, Paul Simon.

Life is a journey. We're all headed somewhere. I'll look for you in Graceland.

"The Entertainer"

– SCOTT JOPLIN

Should a musician be an artist or an entertainer? In the world of music, it's helpful to be a bit of both.

The question for consideration is, who controls the set list? The artist is motivated by, "What can I do that will bring the audience into a larger appreciation of how I see life?" This could involve virtuosic but unknown music that may be difficult for the audience to comprehend, the musical equivalent of "Eat your cauliflower. It's good for you." The driving force for an entertainer is, "Give the audience what they want, even if they've heard it a million times." Yum, chocolate chip cookies!

During my early years of performing in coffeehouses, bookstores, and art shows, I chose the artistic route—original, solo, fingerstyle guitar only, with an occasional version of "Happy Birthday" by request. That worked well in those settings.

A healing environment is different. It is essential to connect with the audience/patient with whatever music is most meaningful to the people who are present. That requires the ability to cover most anything that may be requested. In a healing situation, the goal is not just entertainment or artistic expression. The aim is to awaken the well-worn neural pathways that have been built by the patient's listening habits. That type of mental stimulation releases endorphins and dopamine, the "feel-good" hormones that aid in healing. Any style of music will engage a listener's brain in a positive way, but the closer I get to their musical sweet spot, the more beneficial the experience will be.

My goal has been to combine the roles of artist and entertainer in the hospital setting. There is room for artistic expression when playing in public spaces such as hallways and lobbies. The music goes out to everyone within earshot. Relaxing, instrumental music in public spaces lets people know that live music is available. It prompts an invitation to a more personal expression, *Can you come into the room? We'd love to hear some music.*

To make sure I'm ready to play music in a one-on-one situation, I have worked diligently to expand my repertoire. One never knows what song or style will be most meaningful. Early on in my experience, I was asked, "Do you know any Celtic tunes?" The closest I could get at that time was, "Where the Streets Have No Name" by U2—a far cry from "The Fields of Athenry." Another time, two daughters asked if I could play some Spanish music. "Daddy loves flamenco music so much he installed a speaker in the shower so he could listen to it first thing every morning." The best I could do was a half-remembered arrangement of "Malaguena" by Charo, the *cuchi-cuchi* girl.

Over the years, I've done my best to understand the language of music and its ever-increasing dialects. The more I take time to listen to the small nuances of this language, the better I become at communicating and connecting using a unique blend of art and entertainment.

As a side note, there are some limitations. A handful of times I've been asked to sing something by Beyonce or Celine Dion. When I respond with a falsetto "To the left, to the left" or "My heart will go on," first there's a laugh then the *Maybe we better try a different song* look.

Playing at a hospital bedside can feel a little weird at times. It's like walking into a person's bedroom. But it is in this setting that music becomes very personal; there is no physical or electronic distance between the sender and receiver. The hospital room becomes the perfect venue, setting the stage for the music that resonates most deeply with the patient. Every seat is front row; every song is heart to heart.

"We Are Climbing Jacob's Ladder"

– AFRICAN AMERICAN SPIRITUAL

I knocked on the door. Inside the darkened hospital room were two middle-aged women, apparently daughters, sitting quietly on either side of the bed. Between them was an older woman, their mother, unresponsive with eyes shut. On numerous occasions, nurses have told me to never hesitate to talk or interact with an unresponsive person. Hearing is the last thing to go.

"What kind of music would she enjoy?"

The older daughter turned toward me and said, "Mother was religiously affiliated. Do you know any camp songs? Do you know 'We are Climbing Jacob's Ladder'?"

I began with "Jacob's Ladder," then continued to "This Little Light of Mine," "Michael Row the Boat Ashore," and several others. My experience from Methodist summer camp was serving me well! After fifteen minutes, I said goodbye and quietly went back into the hallway.

Two minutes later, the nurse manager found me, touched my shoulder, and said, "You just sang that woman into heaven."

This was early in my hospital experience and I didn't fully understand the significance of what she was communicating. Did the camp music cause some kind of transcendent experience?

She saw the puzzled look on my face. "The woman you just played for died right after you left."

Stunned shock. At that time, that was the closest I had been to a person passing away.

Later that day, the chaplain caught up with me. "Sometimes when people are near the end, hearing music and having loved ones near will allow them to relax and let go. I've seen situations when a person will hang on until that last distant friend or relative arrives. It's funny, but I think we have more control over our moment of departure than we realize."

"Folsom Prison Blues"

– JOHNNY CASH

One day early in my time as an artist-in-residence, the chaplain asked if I could go to a particular room and play for the patient. He added, "The whole family is there." I thanked him and thought, *What a tremendously supportive family*. At this point in my hospital experience, I didn't yet understand the significance of that phrase.

When I entered the room, a dozen or more people were surrounding a non-responsive woman in the bed.

"What kind of music does she enjoy?"

A woman I took to be the oldest daughter answered. "Country music. She's a big Johnny Cash fan. Do you know 'Folsom Prison'?"

This is perfect, I thought. *I know all the words to that one.*

After the iconic intro riff, we heard the train coming down the line. Everything was going well. A few somber faces melted into faint smiles.

In the middle of the second verse, a nurse walked in and stood beside the bed. She felt for a pulse, then placed her stethoscope gently on the woman's chest. She turned to the oldest daughter and whispered. The daughter began crying and whispered to the person next to her.

Everyone in the room knew she was gone. They gathered closer together, each one connected to this beloved woman in a different way. She had been a sister, mother, grandmother, aunt, and dear friend, the sun at the center of their orbit.

Musically, I was traveling on a train that was moving "a little farther down the line." When I saw the first whisper, I moved that train to a low-speed siding.

A calm, floating series of chords followed. Love, empathy, and sorrow flowed through the room like a gentle stream. The healing sound of music washed over hugs, tears, and whispers.

Did a toe-tapping country tune bring the resolution that allowed this woman to let go? Maybe. Was it the presence of a loving family? Maybe.

Regardless of the cause, mom was gone and now the world was different.

"Go Rest High on that Mountain"

– VINCE GILL

I was walking toward the nurses' station when a lady stepped into the hall, smiled, and asked, "Can you come in here?"

There was an unresponsive man in the bed who I assumed was her husband. But she seemed pretty chipper for a person whose spouse was in such dire condition.

She asked, "Can you play 'Go Rest High on That Mountain'?"

When I hear that question, I know there will be tears. Vince Gill wrote this beautiful tribute for his brother. I don't know all the background, but the lyrics tell the tale of a man's earthly struggles while the singer sings him into eternity. It is a very deep and powerful song.

I found the song sheet in my database and did my best to sound like Vince Gill. Yes, there were tears.

On the small couch in the room was a rumpled pillow, blanket, and sheets. I asked the woman if she had spent the night.

"No, my friend did," she said. The two of them had been taking turns staying with this fellow for the past several days. She went on to tell me that Pete, the man in the bed, was a mutual friend. The three of them had worked together at the Ohio Historical Society for many years.

"He was quite a guy. He grew up in Pomeroy, a small river town in southeastern Ohio. He was orphaned at 10 and sent to live with his grandparents, but they didn't want him and treated him poorly. It wasn't long before he ran away to his aunt's house. She already had six mouths to feed but was willing to take him in. As you can imagine, it was a hardscrabble life, and he was pretty much on his own. When he was big enough, he lied about his age and got into the army a little after his seventeenth birthday. After completing his service, he made his way to Columbus and got a job at the Historical Society as a groundskeeper. He eventually made peace with his past.

"Pete was always thinking of others. He retired and returned to Pomeroy and applied for a $14,000 grant from the State of Ohio. When the money came through, he used it to clean up a pond and turned it into a recreation area where kids can fish. He really had a heart of gold.

"Would you do 'It is Well with My Soul'?" She held his hand as I sang this classic hymn. When it was over, she said, "He feels cold. I'm going to get a nurse."

Sure enough, during those few minutes, Pete had passed into eternity.

A short time later, the chaplain found me and said, "John, the timing was perfect. I had just prayed with them. Then you came in and sang him into heaven."

The music he's hearing now just got a whole lot better! was the first thing that popped into my head. The second thing was *What an amazing person!* He lived humbly and never forgot where he came from. Many children will enjoy a beautiful, sunny day beside a pond thanks to this man's generosity.

"Missing You"

– DIANA ROSS

Can we see into another's world?

Pre-COVID, High Tea was a wonderful volunteer activity. Every Wednesday, a group of women, some retired, some stay-at-home moms, would gather in the Family Lobby of the cancer floor. This crew broke into teams and made sure that each patient on the floor received a red rose in a stem vase and was offered, within dietary restrictions, pastries and tea. There was also live music.

On one High Tea Wednesday, Jean, the piano player, and I were doing our standard fare of pop and jazz tunes. Directly in front of the lobby, a group of teenagers had gathered. They appeared to be sixteen or seventeen years old, maybe younger. They were waiting for an elevator. All the guys had oversized wallets chained to their sagging pants. The girls were decked out in flashy street garb.

The rumble of their conversation was inappropriately loud for a hospital. I was thinking, *Kids these days! Don't they know there are sick people here trying to rest?*

Then, like a swelling siren from the center of this storm, I heard the voice of a young man, a cry, a moan, a drawn-out wail, "I miss my Mama!"

All conversation stopped. The elevator arrived. They stepped aboard and were gone.

Lord, help me see and empathize with pain in whatever age, apparel, color, or culture it comes.

"Don't Think Twice, It's All Right"

– BOB DYLAN

One Saturday morning in October, I sat down for breakfast with an actual newspaper. Yes, an actual paper-and-ink newspaper! I turned to my "go to" section, the comics. Directly across the page were the obituaries. There I saw a familiar face.

A gentleman I had played for on numerous occasions had lost his battle with cancer. He was a big fan of 50s and 60s folk music and especially enjoyed the Kingston Trio and Bob Dylan. Often after I would finish one of his favorite songs, he would look me in the eye and say, "John, how do they do that?"

His obituary confirmed my observations. His early years were spent in a small town in southeast Ohio, not far from where I grew up. In high school he had numerous athletic achievements. This was followed by many professional and charitable accolades. There were tears in my breakfast bowl that morning.

Unexpectedly, a few weeks later, I received an email from his wife. Below is a slightly edited version of our correspondence:

> John,
>
> My husband, B., loved hearing you play while undergoing his weekly infusions. On one of the last days that he was there, he asked you to come in while I was there. He asked you to sing a few of his favorites ("City of New Orleans" and two more). The last one was rather sad, and he started to cry a little. I would love to know which song that was if you have any recollection—it may have been one you had played for him before.
>
> Anyway, B. passed away. I think of that wonderful session with you and can't help wondering if that song had some hidden meaning—that he knew the end was near. He and I had been college sweethearts and married for almost 59 years. He was an exceptional achiever in athletics, personal relations, law, etc.
>
> Sorry to go on like this, but your music gave him comfort and happiness.
>
> Thank you so very much.
>
> N.

N,

Thank you for contacting me. I saw B.'s obituary. Of course, that made me sad, but at the same time it was great to read of the many wonderful accomplishments in his life. None of that was surprising. I knew he was an exceptional person the first time I met him.

I probably played for B. a half dozen times or more. During our times together, he always asked for folk music and would often request "anything by Bob Dylan." I'm fairly sure these are the songs I played during our last time together: "City of New Orleans" by Arlo Guthrie, "MTA" by the Kingston Trio (I played "MTA" for him almost every time I saw him), and "Don't Think Twice" by Bob Dylan. That one may have caused the sadness. The gist of it is, I'm moving on down the road.

One of my favorite memories of B. is that almost every time I saw him, I would finish a song and he would get this reflective look on his face and say, "How do they do that? How does a person come up with such amazing words? Where do they find music that can speak to so many people? How do they do that?"

This inevitably led to conversations about the awe-inspiring act of human creativity in its many forms. He was a great thinker, full of thoughtful questions and significant insights. Most of our discussions would end with him shaking his head in a bemused way and saying, "Amazing, simply amazing."

The week after I saw B.'s obituary, I was feeling a little sad going to the infusion area and knowing that he wouldn't be there. About halfway through my time that day, I sat down to play for a middle-aged man. He said, "Do you know 'City of New Orleans'?" I figured B. was listening in.

Thanks again for contacting me, and I pray that you will experience God's comfort during this difficult time.

John

Oh John,

You did remember him—how special to know that! You are exactly right about the 3 songs you played for him while I was there. It was the last one that meant so much more to him because he seemed to sense something that he wouldn't share with me. He was always like that: sheltering everyone else from his pain. It has taken me a while to realize that his passing was a release for him, to end the pain and finally rest. My grief and sadness are nothing compared to his suffering. You helped him so much.

What you are doing for these patients is beyond any help they are getting from the medical treatments. I wish you a long and satisfying life—continuing to give so much will certainly be repaid to you many times over. Thank you for being with B. and for giving me more insight into his experiences there when I couldn't be with him.

N.

My times with B were a wonderful privilege. Music created a powerful point of connection, but it was his gift of insightful conversation that was truly an act of creativity.

"Birthday"

– THE BEATLES

My phone dinged, a message appeared: *My guitar friend, I am at the last phase of my life. Hospice phase that is. Tomorrow is my early bday. Food comes at 7:30pm you are soooo welcome. Chinese food but not your usual stuff. If not, come other times. Let me know so I can save you a portion when you stop by after the bday... bring your guitar.*

A text from my artist, photographer, all-round-good and interesting friend. When I responded, he told me his actual birthday was a few weeks after the planned celebration, but he wasn't sure he would be available on that date.

We had met in the Rad-Onc lobby several months earlier. The first time we crossed paths, he was sitting quietly, writing, I thought, in a small notebook. I was serenading the world's biggest Elvis fan. After about twenty minutes, he stepped across the lobby and gave the patient a sketch he had made of the two of us. It was a nice line drawing of her enjoying song after song of Elvis's greatest hits. A brief "wow and thanks" conversation followed, then Victor was called for his treatment.

Over the months, we ran into each other numerous times. Victor told me that his mother was Japanese and his father was Vietnamese. His father had worked with the US Army during the Vietnam war, and immediately after the war, the family was relocated to Hawaii.

Growing up in that tropical paradise had instilled in him a love of nature, especially the vivid colors of the Hawaiian flora. This love led, naturally enough, to a serious interest in photography. He had a deep understanding of the technical aspects of light and color plus a good eye for capturing well-balanced images. His specialty was photographing flowers and outdoor scenes.

Victor was always interesting and cheerful, even though he was obviously in physical discomfort. The cancer was taking a huge toll on his body. He was not interested in talking about his disease. His attitude was, *This is just something I'm going through, not too big of a deal, just a part of life.*

However, the disease was preventing him from doing photography the way he liked. He loved nature but couldn't get to the places and things he wanted to photograph. Instead of regretting this loss, he bought a sketch book, and when we first met, he was just beginning to experiment with drawing.

Over the weeks, Victor gave me a tour of his sketch book. It was full of plants and portraits. With each turn of a page, his progress was apparent. In a few short months, he had advanced from monochrome line drawings to incredibly detailed depictions, adding color along the way.

"How do you do that?" I asked.

"Simple," he replied. "I just go someplace—a park, a coffee shop, a waiting room—and watch people. I draw what I see."

More than drawing, Victor was able to capture mood, emotion, and action in an incredibly unique way. Some art gives a particularly good outward impression. Victor's art went deep, way beneath the surface. He had a highly refined style of folk art, something of an Asian-influenced version of Elijah Pierce or Aminah Robinson. It seemed that some of this depth was born from his natural perceptiveness and insight into human nature, but perhaps his natural insight had been honed by his current physical circumstances. Can a simple line drawing convey empathy? Can a flash of color convey personality? Yes.

I was the first to arrive for his early birthday party. When I knocked, I received a cheery "Come in, the door is open!"

The front room of the townhouse was filled with a double bed and a twin bed. Victor was kneeling between them, his elbows on the single bed, knees on the floor and feet on the double bed. He explained in an unapologetic manner that he needed to stay in this position much of the time due to his "current medical situation." He made no mention of pain or discomfort.

The next guest to arrive was Victor's nephew, a bright-eyed young boy probably ten years of age. My friend carefully guided this lad through several three-ring binders full of superhero trading cards. The cards were beautiful, artistic, and carefully displayed in ultra-clear, nine to a page, double-sided pockets. Each section of the binders was arranged in appropriate set groupings. He explained the significance of each card and instructed his nephew in their care. "Always put the cards back in the proper place. Don't get them mixed up. You can take the cards out one at a time to look at them but always put them back in the same pocket where you found them." It was a sweet expression of love as he entrusted this prized collection to the boy's safekeeping. At this party, the person being celebrated gave the gifts.

As more folks arrived, I quickly realized that I had been invited to a very select gathering of family and friends. It also became apparent that I was the only non-Vietnamese speaker in the room.

The sun in the center of this constellation of care was "Mama." Mama and Victor's mother had become friends when he was a young boy. She was a professional hospice caregiver and had cared for many people, including several celebrities who had retired to Hawaii. She had even accompanied one client to England to visit the Queen! Now she had come from Hawaii to take care of Victor as she had taken care of his mother, who had passed away in 2016. Mama was obviously a very caring person, a kind and gentle spirit.

As promised, the food was the good stuff, not the "usual stuff." As I was filling my plate, Mama, with a slight twinkle in her eye, asked if I would like some red sauce. Other folks there were pouring generous quantities of this mysterious concoction onto their mounds of rice and vegetables.

I was onto her trick. "Are you trying to set me on fire?"

"Oh no, no," she laughed. "Just a dot."

I added a dot, mixed it with my heaping pile of rice and veggies, then took a bite. Flames did not literally come out of my nose, but one more dot may have been sufficient to start a small forest fire. It was very tasty... in moderation.

After dinner, Victor asked me to get out my guitar. Mama requested a country song that I hadn't played before, adding, "This is my favorite song!" We looked it up online, found the words and chords, and with help, did a presentable rendition. There were more requests for upbeat pop and country tunes, then Victor asked for "the song by that Hawaiian guy" ("Wonderful World" by Israel Kamakawiwo'ole). Again, this was Mama's favorite song! I think every song was her favorite. Everyone joined in and sang along.

I could see Victor was beginning to tire, so I said, "How about one more?"

"Sure, you pick," he said.

I began playing the most appropriate song I could think of, James Taylor's "Shower the People You Love with Love."

Earlier, Victor had been moving around the room, talking and laughing; at this point, he was once again kneeling between the beds in the front room. About a verse into the song, he pulled himself up, crawled over the single bed, took Mama in his arms, and began dancing, a graceful expression of his love and appreciation.

Tears streamed down every face as the dance continued. This was the highlight of his living memorial service/birthday party.

Music made the moment as well as opening the door for a privileged peek into the world of an incredible person. One of the last things Victor said to me summed up his approach to life, "I love flowers but I don't need them after I'm gone. Let's enjoy them now, while we're all together."

A few short weeks later, just short of his calendar birthday, he danced into eternity.

"Softly as I Leave You"

– ELVIS PRESLEY

I was standing in the Palliative Care hallway when the door directly across from me cracked open. From inside the dimly lit room, a hand emerged, and the extended index finger summoned me in.

As I stepped into this twilight world, the woman who had beckoned sat down in a chair facing the bed to my immediate right. I turned and looked. There was a middle-aged man, her husband, lying with eyes closed.

He feebly asked, “Can I play your guitar?”

I carefully placed it on his chest and stood close by, unsure that he had the strength to hold it in place. Slowly and weakly his left hand formed a C chord—a faint, muted strum. Then ever so carefully an F chord—a light half strum. He continued between the two chords for a minute or so, making adjustments and improving the sound.

The phone rang. His wife answered. “Yes, he’s right here.” She crossed the room and gently brought the phone to his ear.

“Hi… not too well… I’ve got a guitar… listen.” He began to play the chords again, but this time he was quietly singing a song by Elvis Presley, “Softly as I Leave You.”

That was as far as he could make it. He motioned the guitar in my direction. His wife continued to hold the phone to his ear. “I know… I love you too…”

I quietly left the room.

I recognized the song as one Elvis had popularized but I wasn’t familiar with the story behind it. When I got home, I looked it up. I found a video of Elvis introducing “Softly as I Leave You.” As he tells it, it’s a song about a man who is dying. His wife has been with him in the hospital for three days. She climbs into bed beside him and falls asleep, and as he feels himself passing away, he doesn’t want to wake her. A song was born. Amazingly, I had just seen a version of this play out in real life.

Several weeks later, the hospital forwarded me an email.

Dear Mr. Morgan,

We have never met and probably never will, as I'm a Florida resident. However, without knowing it, you have made a lasting impression on me. My brother R. was a patient in the palliative care unit. On May 6, you were strumming your guitar and walking down the hallway. When he heard you, he asked if you would let him play your guitar. He taught himself how to play years ago and often played to relieve tension as well as for enjoyment. While he was strumming your guitar, I just happened to call him, and he told me what he was doing. During our phone call, he sang "Softly as I Leave You" for me... and then he told me he was very tired and that he was sorry, but he had to go and then goodbye. He passed away a short time after we hung up. That song and conversation will be with me for as long as I live!

R. was a very special brother and I miss him beyond words. I want to thank you for giving him the pleasure of playing the guitar for the last time and for giving me the most beautiful parting gift imaginable, his singing to me. God bless you always.

R's sister,

"Betty"

Sometimes the most helpful thing we can do is simply show up.

"The Gambler"

– KENNY ROGERS

"Can you play for this patient?" The palliative nurse and social worker had just stepped out of a room. The door was closing behind them as the light in the room grew dim. "She's actively dying."

I took a deep breath and opened the door. Family members were gathered around the bed, a son on either side and a daughter at the foot. They were gently massaging the feet and shoulders of their mother as tears rolled down their cheeks. Surrounding the siblings were spouses and grandsons.

When a person is actively dying, facial muscles slacken, the mouth gapes, breathing is slow and sometimes labored, eyes are closed. This much-loved woman was exhibiting all these symptoms. It appeared she would be leaving this world at any moment.

The daughter spoke first.

"She loves gospel music and hymns. Do you know 'Amazing Grace'?"

The mood was somber as I sang the familiar lyrics.

"Could you play 'Lord of the Dance'?"

The title threw me for a minute, then I remembered. This song is built on the melody of the Shaker classic "Simple Gifts." We found the lyrics and sang.

When I finished, the oldest son spoke up. "Do you know any Kenny Rogers songs? Her all-time favorite song is 'The Gambler'."

"The Gambler" is a song that I play with caution at the hospital, only upon request. It tells the tale of a gambler who passes along his advice for living, then he dies in his sleep. That seemed a little too close to the current situation, but I've found that there is always a reason for the songs people request.

I recruited one of the grandsons to hold my tablet. Feeling the sadness in the room, I thought it best to focus my eyes and thoughts on the lyrics, as a preventative measure. It's hard to sing through tears.

As I sang the last chorus, I noticed some movement coming from the bed. I looked up. I believe in the power of music, I've experienced it, and yet, I was startled by what I saw in front of me.

The actively dying woman was sitting up, her eyes wide open, a huge smile on her face. She was waving her arms in the air and shaking both legs. She was dancing in bed as she declared, "That's my favorite song!"

The atmosphere in the room was immediately transformed from tears to joyous laughter!

She looked around the room at each adoring face. "I love you all!" She focused intently on each of her children and their spouses as she repeated, "I love all of you so much."

Teary replies. "We love you too, Mom. We're here for you."

Her gaze slowly shifted to the grandson holding the tablet, and calling him by name, she said, "You've grown into such a fine young man!"

Her children told me their mom was a huge Elvis fan and asked for a gospel song he had recorded. "Take my Hand, Precious Lord" was followed by "Can't Help Falling in Love." Mom relaxed, drifted off, and was once again beyond their reach.

In an attempt to bring her back, the younger son asked for a bluegrass tune—his mom had grown up in North Carolina. Someone immediately called out, "Rocky Top." Okay, a classic moonshine song isn't a normal request for a palliative patient, but a request is a request. There's always a reason.

Incredibly, this rollicking bluegrass foot stomper brought Mom back to the land of the living. Again, her first words were to her family, telling them all how much she loved them. This time her voice was slightly stronger as the family leaned towards her, tuning into her every word.

First in view was her oldest son. "I remember the day you were born. It was wonderful! You were such a ball of red hair, kicking and crying. Dad said, 'This boy is going to be a good one!'" Next, she spotted her daughter. "I can still picture you on the floor in a diaper, kicking and pitching a fit. I loved every minute of it!"

Moments later, a young couple walked into the room. They had the glow of newlyweds. Moving toward the head of the bed, they announced, "We're here, Grandma." She looked at them and with a prophetic authority said, "Oh, I love you so much! God is going to bless you with a little girl, and when He does, He will look down and smile and be so happy."

The blessings continued as her gaze fell on each one in the room. Landing on my unfamiliar face, she stared, bemused for a moment, and then said, "Thank you for the music. God bless you."

Drawing near, the daughter tenderly wrapped her arm around her mother. She asked, "Mom, what would you like us to sing to celebrate your entrance into your eternal reward?"

Mom considered the question, looked her daughter in the eyes, and said, "Let's save that for later." Once again, tears and laughter overflowed as the gravity and wit of this woman reached into our hearts.

When the room grew quiet again, someone said, "Mom, you were such a great teacher. Your students always loved you." Earlier in my visit, one of the children had mentioned that their mother had a thirty-year career as a teacher of grades three through six.

Mom addressed the room. "When I started, one of the older teachers told me to always take care how I treat my students. 'They think the world of you. Don't let them down,' she told me." She paused. "That scared me to death!"

"Those kids were so fortunate," the daughter replied. "They got a piece of you. But we are even more blessed—we got a whole big chunk of you. Is there a song we can all sing for you?"

Mom's last request was "The Old Rugged Cross." The family quietly joined in as she slid back into a deep sleep. Later that evening, she passed peacefully into eternity.

This saintly woman had raised a loving family, had a formative role in the lives of hundreds of children, and in a few brief minutes, had profoundly touched the heart of a random guitar player. What a beautiful, rich lesson: Live well, die well. Use your life to build a legacy.

"Time After Time"

– CYNDI LAUPER

Enjoying music as part of your daily routine is a component of a well-balanced mental diet; wake up to music, sing in the shower or car, whistle while you work, or hum while you walk. All have mental and emotional benefits.

On a societal level, music is a common thread running through many of our major life events: birthdays, weddings, funerals, and religious services. It draws people together and forms community. Invisible vibrating air molecules touch us in settings large and small.

One Thursday afternoon, I rounded the corner by the south nurses' station and heard a familiar voice. "John, you turn up everywhere!" It was Kathy, a friend I hadn't seen in many years.

When I began performing as a solo fingerstyle guitarist, it was mostly at bookstores and coffee shops. After the release of my first CD, I decided to find larger venues in hopes of expanding my audience. Between the internet and some door knocking, I landed several art show gigs in central and northeast Ohio. The largest and most prestigious of these was Winterfair in Columbus. On the first weekend in December, this annual event draws hundreds of the finest artists from across the country. The daily schedule was far more demanding than a two-hour bookstore gig. Each day would begin mid-morning and run till evening. Also, much better than a bookstore, the artsy audience would be in the thousands, not the low double digits.

I set up my equipment at one end of the food court, a place where people could grab a treat and rest their feet. My sound system was connected to the overhead PA providing a sprinkling of music over the huge convention hall. This wasn't a concert, just a little sonic ambiance, jazzed up Christmas carols and relaxing originals. Some people would stop and talk; others gave a wave or a nod.

Late on Saturday afternoon, I heard a conversation taking place at a table directly behind me. I could only catch snippets of what was being said. "California... concert... acoustic guitar... much better..."

In a somewhat fatigued state, my mind immediately raced to the worst-case scenario. Obviously, this couple had recently been to a much better acoustic concert in California and were now being subjected to the music of some Ohio bumpkin. Early in my solo career, self-confidence wasn't my forte. This was at a time when several fingerstyle players were gaining national prominence. I had no idea if I even fit in the Columbus music scene.

A few minutes later, I heard the couple get up to leave. Instead of disappearing into the crowd. they walked around and introduced themselves. Turns out my eavesdropping was less than accurate. Don and Kathy had been in southern California the weekend before and they had attended an acoustic guitar concert, but instead of my worst-case assumption, they were actually enjoying the music of this bumpkin. As the conversation continued, they purchased a CD and took my contact info. A week later, I was booked for their upcoming wedding reception.

Their reception was a grand event, loads of friends and family enjoying each other's company, lots of laughter, tables loaded with food and drink, all taking place in a well-appointed country club.

Don and Kathy's reception was fully fun and festive. My musical goal for this type of setting is to tune in to the vibe of the tribe and make it come alive.

A few years later, I ran into Don and Kathy again. It may have been at another art show. Life was going well and there was now a baby girl in their carriage.

Today, a half dozen years later, our paths crossed again, this time in the hospital.

Our meeting on the cancer floor was much different than the wedding celebration. It surprised me when Kathy said, "I've been thinking about you. I lost your contact information and wanted to get in touch, then suddenly you appear." We laughed.

She was on this floor spending time with her mom, who was receiving palliative cancer care. When we entered the room, Kathy's mom was resting in bed. Seeing the guitar and listening to a few songs brought back sweet memories of the wedding day. The music and conversation provided a moment of relief during this heart-rending time.

It was only a few weeks until I received a call from Kathy. "Mom passed; can you play for her memorial service?"

The answer is easy. The performance is not. Being asked to play music for a memorial is truly an honor, but there is the underlying fear that the emotions at such an occasion will be overwhelming.

I'm reminded of the words of Reverend Hughey Jones, a longtime friend of my family, "We have all been together in times of great joy. It is only right that we are together today." In the strength of being together there is grace for the musician to unite and comfort.

The importance of sharing grief publicly cannot be overstated. During times of great loss, difficult and complex emotions rise to the surface. Music can bring focus and release to unformed sorrow too deep to be spoken. It provides time for reflection and permission for tears, opening the door to emotional healing.

It is a holy experience to hear friends and family join their voices in a song of memory and respect. I am thankful for the times I've been invited into this beauty and brokenness.

A measure of minutes,
come days in a row.
We walk 'cross the stage,
The river still flows.
- JDM

As a side note, Reverend Jones wrote a letter to be read at his own funeral. It began like this: Hello, friends! Thanks for coming. I wish I could be there with you all, but as you know, I'm in a much better place now!

7

Fandom

"Can't Help Falling in Love"

– ELVIS PRESLEY

"Fan" is the handy abbreviation of "fanatic." There are sports fans, car fans, and fans of collecting Pez dispensers. Naturally, when it comes to music, there is no shortage of fanatical fans.

I was in the radiation lobby when a lady, Kay, walked in with her husband. "Oh my, Barry Manilow!"

Another lady, Diane, had come for treatment a week before. She had asked what Barry Manilow songs I knew. The answer at that time was *zilch, zero, zip*. She had given me a list of her favorites, and I had done my homework. There were now two beloved Barry Manilow songs in my database.

I was in the middle of "Mandy" when Kay arrived. Both ladies were thrilled and asked, "What else do you know by him?" My only other Barry tune was, "I Write the Songs." There were sighs and hearts aflutter.

Kay and Diane were two kindred spirits drawn together by their love of Barry Manilow and his music. They loved all things Barry, his live stage productions were "fabulous," his voice was "dreamy," his songs, "so romantic." Both ladies were exuberant, but I detected more than a little eye-rolling by both husbands. The conversation quickly turned to:

K: "Did you see him when he played in Columbus?"

D: "Oh yes!"

K: "What about Cleveland and Cincinnati?"

D: "Of course. And we've made multiple trips to Las Vegas and New York."

K: "How wonderful. So have we. We're going back to Las Vegas when we get through with this round of cancer treatment."

Even though this conversation sounds like a case of escalating one-upmanship, it really wasn't. These were true believers celebrating their mutual musical hero.

K: "At last count, we've seen him thirty-two times."

D: "We've seen him fifty-six times. I thought that was great until I went to one of the meet-and-greets. I had to wait in line for forty-five minutes. I was so excited to tell him that we had been to fifty-six of his concerts. Then I overheard the lady in front of me say that she had been to three hundred and twenty-four of his shows. That took the wind out of my sails."

If I can borrow one of Barry's lines, "music and passion were always in fashion" with these ladies. Is music able to reach deep and touch something significant inside of us? I think these fans would have a strong opinion on that topic.

Barry has fans, but Elvis has FANS!

The impact of Elvis Aaron Presley on the American music scene is unparalleled. Enough books have been written, movies produced, and souvenirs manufactured to fill a small town. Who would live in that town? It could be entirely populated by Elvis impersonators and its suburbs inhabited by loyal fans.

Plenty has been written about every facet of Elvis's life, I would like to share a little about the folks I've met who constitute the long-trailing tail of this comet.

"Return to Sender" (Elvis)

I was invited into a room on the cancer floor. A man was in the bed; his wife and two daughters were sitting on the couch and chairs. When I asked what kind of music he liked, he answered without hesitation.

"Anything by Elvis."

I clicked on my tablet and picked one of my favorites, "Return to Sender." Before I got through the first verse, everyone in the room but me was laughing. I stopped and jokingly said, "Hey, what's the problem? I'm not that bad!"

One of the daughters, still chuckling and gesturing toward her dad, said, "He's a mailman!" The song about a letter of apology refused by an upset girlfriend was the perfect start for our time together.

On another day, I knocked on the door of a woman who called herself a baby boomer. Musically, she asked for "Anything, as long as it's mostly rock and roll."

After I played several Beatles tunes and something else from that era, she asked for one more. "How about 'Hound Dog' by Elvis?"

This is not an obscure song, but it's one I hadn't played at the hospital in years. Of all the songs I played for her that day, this one seemed to have the most connection to her teen years. Joyful toes were tapping under the sheets.

Near the end of my day, I was directed to a room by the nurse who I jokingly called my agent. She always has an ear out for patients who would benefit from music. "I think this lady would really enjoy hearing you," she told me.

When I entered, a woman in her mid-70s, looking very prim and proper (pay no attention to the less-than-stylish hospital gown), told me she liked bluegrass and church music. After several bluegrass hymns, she commented, "You play a lot like Elmer. He used to do all that fancy stuff."

It turns out she was part of a very musical family in Virginia. She was the youngest daughter. Back in the day, two of her brothers formed a band and drafted her as the backup singer/guitarist. Her oldest brother was the most serious musician in the band. "He played with great intensity and could play mandolin just like Bill Monroe. Elmer was slightly younger and a little flashier. He really liked to get the crowd into it."

She got very animated, as she reminisced about their musical travels in the mountains of Virginia. Toward the end of our conversation, she said, "You know what I really liked? Boogie woogie."

Her only regret was that she had never seen Elvis in person. "Do you know 'Hound Dog'? I would really love to hear that!"

So, after a long time of no "Hound Dog," *bang*, twice in one day! Mere coincidence, an alignment of the stars, mere happenstance? Whatever it was, Elvis was in the House.

The real beauty of what took place that day was seeing two women of different generations awaken positive memories by hearing songs of their youth.

Were these folks Elvis fans? Yes, but not in the first circle of fandom.

Kissed by the King

It was a Thursday afternoon. The lady reclining in the infusion chair was relaxed, quietly receiving a blood transfusion. I asked what kind of music she would enjoy.

She immediately sat up—almost jumped up—and answered, "Anything by Elvis! I like all kinds of music, but Elvis is my absolute favorite." In an instant, this mellow senior citizen had transformed into an enthusiastic teenager.

Calling on my trusty tablet and in my best Elvis voice, I did a rendition of "I Can't Help Falling in Love With You."

When I finished, she asked, "Do you want to see a picture of when Elvis kissed me?"

"When Elvis kissed you? I sure do!"

She went on, "I was 17 at the time, and now I'm 79." She pulled out her phone and, sure enough, there was Elvis, wrapped around an attractive young girl. When I say "wrapped around," that is no figure of speech. This was no little "peck on the cheek." It was a "hunka, hunka burning love," fully engaged kiss on the lips.

"Wait a minute," I said, "there weren't any cell phones when you were 17."

"You are absolutely right," she replied. "But as soon as I got one, I put this picture on it. Do you want to see the video?" Again, she pulled up her phone and showed me a 30-second, high-quality video clip of Elvis performing no more than five feet from the camera, the fringe of his white jump suit flying in every direction. Sweat was practically dripping off the screen. Even on the tiny phone video, the energy was palpable.

"OK, what's the story here?"

She broke into a huge grin as she told me how she and her girlfriend, both seventeen at the time, had convinced their parents to let them drive from Columbus to Las Vegas where Elvis had a standing gig at the Sands Hotel. A friend had loaned them a high-quality video camera. When they arrived, they told the maître d' the closer he got them to the front of the stage, the better his tip would be. The master of the house had no trouble seating two cute teens in the front row, mere feet from the stage. Twice during the show, Elvis pulled my new friend up on stage and gave her the memory of a lifetime.

By the end of her story, this jolly grandmother was a giggling teen. A few more songs by the King, and I was on my way.

Was this lady the biggest Elvis fan ever? No, not quite. Neither was the first Elvis impersonator I met at the hospital.

Singing with the King

I was playing music in the hall of the cancer floor when a man stuck his head out of a doorway, obviously interested in the music. When I finished what I was playing, he introduced himself and told me how much he and his wife were enjoying what they were hearing. He told me that he was a musician also—an Elvis impersonator.

"What do you know by Elvis?" he asked.

I gave him a couple of options.

"Come with me," he said, and we headed into the room. He introduced me to his wife, who was resting in bed. He gave me a look and "1, 2, 3, hit it!"

He had a great Elvis-like voice, something that isn't always the case with impersonators. First came "I Can't Help Falling in Love with You." His wife lit up! This was followed by "Don't be Cruel" and "Love Me Tender." The performance ended with her applause and his spot-on "Thank you, thank you very much."

Elvis hadn't quite left the building. He and I walked back into the hall, and I asked him how in the world he got started as an Elvis impersonator. He explained that a series of connections from his day job as a CPA led to him doing fund raisers as an Elvis impersonator. “I have a couple of the outfits with all the trimmings. We do an annual fundraiser that sells out every year.”

I had to chuckle. Most of the accountants I know are quiet and unassuming, the kind of folks who wouldn’t think of getting in front of a crowd unless it was to explain some obscure detail of the tax code. Yet here was a man who had broken that stereotype and was now using his talent to raise money for the Nelsonville Opera House. For years he and other community members had been organizing a Legends concert. These local musicians stepped up to the stage performing classic songs by legendary artists. The proceeds of the concert went toward keeping this gem of a venue alive.

As we were talking, a man stepped out of the room directly across the hall. “Could the two of you come in here?”

When we entered, he introduced us to his wife, who immediately exclaimed, “It’s Elvis! We heard you singing but had no idea it was our *very own* Elvis.”

Amazingly, this patient and her husband were also from the Athens area. They were already fans of my newly discovered musical partner. This woman was resting in a hospital bed, unaware that her local musical hero was only a hall’s width away.

We immediately revived our newly concocted show and added “Hound Dog.” Lively applause and smiles all around. “Thank you, thank you very much.”

As we were getting ready to leave, the patient said, “We try to attend the Legends concert every year, but for the last two years, it sold out before we could get tickets.”

"No worries," replied Elvis. "Give me your contact information. I'll make sure you have tickets this year."

It's safe to say that any person in a hospital receiving cancer care is not experiencing their best day. What a difference a little creative diversion can make, singing a few words, playing a few chords connecting the present to the pleasant past, mixing it all together—and you have the recipe for lifting spirits.

Number One Elvis Fan

These folks were all definitely Elvis fans, but none of them compared to a lady I'll call Linda. We first met as she was going through radiation treatment. At first, she would ask for a couple of Elvis songs. As her treatment continued over the weeks, she would request more Elvis songs. Sometimes she would stay after her treatment for a song or two.

This lady's life had not been easy. She had been a single mom raising two boys and working at a tire factory in Akron to support them. There weren't any kind thoughts toward her ex-husband, who had flown the coop. One of the sons lived nearby and, even with a busy life of his own, he was her chauffeur and general caretaker. Unfortunately, he was the "bad" son. When I interjected that he sure seemed like a good guy to me, she disagreed. "No, he's the bad son."

In time, I figured out that her assessment was likely based on the fact that this son, Keith, looked like his dad. The "good" son lived out of town and wasn't able to be directly involved in her care. Whatever the case, mother and son were practiced at the art of direct communication with one another. This made for some prickly and at times humorous conversations.

Linda told me on many occasions that she was Elvis's biggest fan. Her house was decorated with everything Elvis, all kinds of souvenirs, photos, records, CDs, you name it, if it was something Elvis, she had to have one... or two. It goes without saying, she had seen all of his movies and had VHS tapes and DVDs of most of them.

One week while she was receiving treatment, she brought me an Elvis Christmas ornament, dressed in his trademark white-fringed jumpsuit and holding a microphone. "The grandkids don't respect this enough. They keep knocking it off the shelf. I want you to have it. I know you'll take care of it."

She was right. I took it home and put it on my trophy shelf, a shelf in my practice room filled with small handmade pictures and art that I've received from patients and school children.

I was always glad to see Linda and her son Keith. They were both interesting conversationalists, and despite the occasional spats, there was an obvious bond of love between them. I was sorry when it came time for her last treatment—happy for her, sad because I didn't expect to see them in the future.

But surprise! Linda and her son came back to the radiation lobby the following week and for five more weeks after the completion of her treatment. Not for any medical reason. Simply because she loved to hear her music. Now the musical requests changed from "anything by Elvis" to "everything by Elvis." My database already had a significant number of Elvis tunes but a significant number was not enough. Our all-Elvis concerts would typically last forty-five minutes. Fortunately, the other patients were either fans or very tolerant of a fellow patient's musical taste. A concert of this length took us well beyond "Hound Dog" and "Love Me Tender." I had to explore parts of his catalog I was previously unaware of, songs like "(Let Me Be

Your) Teddy Bear," "I Don't Care if the Sun Don't Shine," and "Big Boss Man."

When I asked Linda how she became such a huge fan she said, "Well, when I was 18, I was living in Akron. My girlfriend and I heard that Elvis was coming to Cleveland. We had to be there! It took some convincing, but our parents let us drive up there to see him. I fell in love with him that night, and I've been in love with him ever since."

At this point in the conversation, she would inevitably review her home decorating choices, which her son verified. "Yep, everything Elvis."

In our many get togethers, I recognized repeated stories and looping conversations, signs of dementia/Alzheimer's. Each week she would tell me about driving to Cleveland and falling in love with the King, and then how her love for Elvis had sustained her when her husband left. "Being a single, working mom with two boys was tough, but we made it through." She often told me that Elvis would always be Number One in her heart—after all, he had the fancy clothes and the sexy moves—but I was a close Number Two in her musical hall of fame. Being number two is fine with me.

The breakdown in memory I witnessed in her conversation was familiar to me. My mom had gone through this same pattern and was then at a point where she couldn't speak. Even though Mom couldn't ask for a song, I would regularly go to her memory care unit and play a few tunes, mostly hymns, and Elvis did also show up there on occasion. Playing for Linda was like being able to do something for my mom that she would enjoy but was unable to request.

A change in circumstances brought our six-week concert series to an end. Linda's son was going to be traveling for several weeks, and it made sense for her to move to an assisted living facility. When Keith returned from his trip, he brought her for one more lobby concert. At this point, her mobility and ability to travel in a car became very difficult. Elvis once again dazzled his fan, but now it looked like this mini Las Vegas run was over.

Coda

Six months after my last all-Elvis concert with Linda, I was playing in the hallway of the cancer floor. Out from the doorway of a room on my right came a familiar face. It was Linda's son, Keith, yes, the "bad" son who was still diligently caring for his now-hospitalized mom. We caught up on his travels for a few minutes as we were standing in the doorway. "You've got to see Madrid. What an amazing city!"

Then the conversation moved to Linda. He told me she had fallen and broken a hip. The doctors were strongly recommending surgery. Suddenly a voice spoke up from inside the room: "I don't want anyone cutting on me!"

"Now, Mom, we've talked about this. If you don't have the surgery, you will be in miserable pain and will die in a few weeks or months. If you have the surgery, we can take pain out of the equation, and you'll live longer and happier. Anyway, John is here, would you like to hear some music?"

"Of course, come on in." I don't normally get in a patient's personal space but on this occasion, I received a warm smile and a little peck on the cheek.

Her son was ready for a break and headed to the cafeteria. She started talking about not wanting to have surgery. I quickly switched the conversation to music, but I took a brief moment to mention that there are some very smart people around here who do a good job of helping people feel better and suggested surgery might be a good option. I played her favorites for about fifteen minutes till Keith returned.

She was visibly tired. One last goodbye, then I headed down the hall.

About a half hour later, Keith caught up with me. "You'll never believe it. Mom has decided to go through with the surgery. The only thing I can attribute that to is the music. Your playing calmed her down enough to make a rational decision. I can't thank you enough."

Linda was one of the most memorable characters in my hospital experience. A tough, self-reliant, somewhat cantankerous woman on the outside with a warm heart on the inside. Her love for Elvis was unwavering.

What to make of all this fandom? There are artists who appear at the right place and at the right time. Their music, presentation, and persona become an icon of the era. They may have the same or more faults, flaws, and shortcomings as the rest of their generation, but they are able to temporarily replace the trials and tedium of everyday life with some flash and excitement. When Barry or Elvis or the pop star of the day is in the building, everything, at least for a while, is going to be all right.

8

"Don't Get Around Much Anymore"

— DUKE ELLINGTON

“Sultans of Swing”

– DIRE STRAITS

Way back in 2007, Terry, who was my student and friend, asked if I could start a jam session. “I don’t want to be in a band, I just want to play music with some people,” he explained.

He figured it would be easy enough for me to get a few people together for a little pickin’ and grinnin’.

At that time, I was teaching guitar lessons five days a week, and several of those days included evenings. The best time for a jam session would be Saturday mornings. With that in mind, it only took me a second to answer Terry with a definitive “No.” That was the same answer I gave him the second and the third time he asked. Persistence is one key to success in the real estate world, and that’s where Terry mastered this skill. When I finally relented, my only thought was, *Let’s give it a spin and see what happens. These things fade out pretty quickly.*

I had no idea that this casual gathering would become an informal institution, a social club, and even a cancer support group, a place where people could replace the tag “cancer patient” with “musician.”

As with any informal gathering, people came and went, but there was aways a core of jammers who came and stayed. Why?

Maybe it’s because of what happens when we get together. Making and sharing music is fun. We welcome and encourage all skill levels. Weekly jamming means steady improvement. We don’t talk politics, and we do support the café, including generous tips for the hard-working baristas.

With those values, it is unlikely—no, impossible—that we will ever sound like the original artists; even so, most of the songs roll smoothly down the tracks. Which isn't to say that there haven't been and will never be any "train wrecks." Fortunately, there are no injuries in a musical train wreck, and it all ends with a laugh.

For a decade, I performed at the Westerville Arts and Music Festival. This was during my solo, instrumental-only, fingerstyle-guitarist phase. In 2012, the fellow doing the booking for the festival told me they weren't hiring any solo artists that year, only bands. A light bulb came on. "I can put together a band. How about a band with fifteen or more guitarists?" The answer was yes, and an annual tradition was born.

The jam has not gone unscathed by cancer. Some jammers have gone through treatment and returned to their normal lives. But as Bob Marley would say, "Good friends we have. Good friends we have lost." This includes John, Jim, Wally, and Robert. More than one memorial service has included a circle of guitarists honoring the memory of a good friend we have lost.

Way back when the jam was only a persistent request, I had no understanding of what was being weighed on the balance scale of life. On one side, my leisurely Saturday mornings; on the other, long-term friendships, the joy of informal music making, many fun musical adventures, generating support for worthy charities, and the value of learning and performing songs that I would never play under any other circumstances.

In previous generations, a social gathering of this sort might have taken the shape of a boys'-night-out bowling team or poker game. Our Tuesday night get-togethers are something different. This type of music making is half party, half concert. It's like being on a team, guys and gals, where everyone plays and everyone wins. There are social, mental, and physical health benefits to playing music, but don't let that secret out. The truth is, it's just plain fun—and who couldn't use a weekly dose of that!

Obviously, we haven't faded out as quickly as I expected. As of this writing, we have been gathering for over fifteen years. From all indications, we're headed straight into the future.

"Take Me Out to the Ball Game"

– JACK NORWORTH AND ALBERT VON TILZER

Music brings people together in strange and unexpected ways. The jam band was invited to play for a cancer survivor event near the Ohio State campus. There were drum circles, singers, art displays, recommended resources, and, most importantly, free food. Underneath one of the large circus tents was a stage set up with a professional sound crew.

On this day, a dozen from the ever-changing lineup of the jam band showed up to play. Halfway through our set, I gave my usual invitation to the audience: "Some of you are sitting there watching us and thinking, *Good grief! I'm as good as those guys. I could do that!* And yes, you are right. We meet weekly in Westerville. You are welcome to join us. If you want more details, see me when we're done."

That usually gets a laugh and sometimes a response.

As we were packing up, a gentleman, probably in his early 80s, walked over to me. After a little chit-chat, he told me how much he enjoyed our performance. Then he asked, "Did you really mean what you said about joining the group?"

"Yes, and here's our audition," I said, touching the first two fingers of my right hand to my left wrist and feeling for a pulse.

He told me that he had grown up in Chicago and had played music most of his life. *Hmmm,* I thought, *perhaps a blues guy.* But his wiry build and manner of speech reminded me of a bluegrass picker, maybe a mandolin or banjo player.

We continued to talk for about half an hour, mostly about music. He briefly mentioned that he had come to this event as a cancer survivor.

As he was turning to leave, he said, "I'm going to come to your group next Tuesday. By the way, I play accordion."

Those words, spoken so casually, stopped me in my tracks.

Many guitarists of a certain age have a specific, semi-delusional image of themselves. It's the image of a twenty-year-old rock guitar god with long flowing hair, a stadium full of adoring fans, and audiences held spellbound by every amazing riff. There is no place in this fantasy world for even the thought of an accordion.

In a popular soft drink commercial from back in my youth, a thirsty eleven-year-old Jimi Hendrix is walking down a street in Seattle. He must choose between two colas. Thankfully, he buys a bottle from the vending machine next to a guitar shop where a Fender Stratocaster catches his eye, saving him from the soda machine across the street—next to an accordion store.

Oh no, what have I done? I have just invited a player of the uncool, outdated accordion into the hangout of the hypothetically hip!

The other folks at the jam weren't exactly sure what to make of Roger on that first Tuesday. Here was a fellow fifteen to twenty years older than the rest of us, and that funny-looking instrument he pulled out of his well-worn suitcase didn't exactly say rock and roll.

Fortunately, Roger was a gem of a man. A retired electrical engineer, he was very intelligent and had a warm smile and a love for people that quickly connected him to the whole group.

On subsequent jam nights while most of us were setting up our gear, he would break out his accordion and play "Take Me Out to the Ball Game," "Roll Out the Barrel," and a medley of classic polka tunes. Once we were set up, he would put his jam song sheets on his music stand and join in on the Beatles, the Eagles, and other eclectic pop, rock, and blues tunes that were on the evening's set list.

One Tuesday, after he had been with us for a month, I said, "Roger, you don't know many of these songs, do you?"

With a wry chuckle, he replied in his distinctive Chicago accent. "John, I've never heard any of these songs! When I was growing up in Chicago, there weren't any guitars there."

Now it was my turn to laugh. Guitar-playing blues musicians had been part of the great northern migration of African Americans since at least 1910.

Roger went on to clarify. "I grew up in a Polish-Catholic neighborhood. In my community, it was accordions and polka, and nothing but accordions and polka. Frankie Yankovic was our rock star."

The first weekend in December, the jam group played for Miracle on Williams Street in Delaware, Ohio. This was an annual Spirit of

Christmas event. Needy families would come to the Williams Street Methodist Church's basement where two large rooms were filled with presents—one room where parents could pick out free presents for their children, the other where children could choose free gifts for their parents.

That year, Miracle on Williams Street took place on a Friday evening and Saturday morning. Roger was delighted to be part of this event and was there both days. Halfway through our three-hour set, we took a fifteen-minute break. Roger asked if he could continue to play. He filled the room with cheerful music while the rest of us ate cookies. It was quite a sight: Roger sitting solo, playing the squeeze box for all it was worth, while sporting a Christmas tie, a red elf hat, and an ear-to-ear grin. This was the first and only time I ever heard "Take Me Out to the Ballgame" and "Roll Out the Barrel" included in a Christmas concert!

While we were inside making music and eating cookies, Mother Nature was busy decorating the landscape with icy wonders. An intense winter storm had gotten ahead of the salt trucks and covered the roads and streets with snow and black ice. A crystal coating of ice glazed the tree branches.

Yipes! An elderly gentleman was going to be driving his boat of a car down a slippery, unplowed highway. What if he slid off the road or spun into the center lane? He was a very independent fellow, so I didn't want to appear overly protective, but he had a sixteen-mile drive ahead of him that was more suited to a dogsled than a car.

I followed Roger at a distance as we headed down Route 23, steady as she goes. When we reached 270, the Columbus outer belt, the road was plowed and clear. I broke off and headed home.

The following morning, we were back in the church basement getting ready for another round of music and Christmas shoppers.

"Roger, I don't know if you noticed, but I was following you last night. I was concerned about the weather."

"John," he chortled, "no need to worry about me. Remember, I grew up in Chicago. I love driving in snow."

Roger continued with the group for a little more than two years. He was having the time of his life playing rock and roll with a bunch of "young" forty-to-sixty-year-old guys and gals. Then his medical issues returned.

He was living with his daughter. She kept in touch with us as his condition worsened. One day she asked if a small group of jammers could stop by for a brief visit. We did, and Roger joyfully pulled out his accordion and joined us for two songs. A month later, his daughter invited us back for an early birthday party. He wasn't feeling well enough to play music this time, but he was well enough to enjoy ice cream and cake. Two weeks later, Roger passed.

Those in the group who were able to attend Roger's memorial service got an expanded view of his life. Not surprisingly, it was a story of love, care, and accomplishment. Roger showed us how to finish well. This hardy Chicago native wasn't afraid of an adventure or of being different; unknown music, icy roads—not a problem.

I can talk about making the most of every day, but Roger lived it. He loved music and people with a beautiful child-like enthusiasm.

Lesson to be learned: Being authentic will always outmatch being cool.

"Just Because"

– ANITA BAKER

One Monday, a middle-aged woman invited me into the room to play music for her mother. The mom was not only battling cancer but was also experiencing an advanced stage of dementia. She was unable to speak; her eyes were open and listlessly observing activity in the room.

The daughter told me that her mom liked guitar music and especially enjoyed instrumental music. After the first song, Mom became much more attentive and focused, and during the ten minutes I was in the room, she was progressively more engaged. When I ran into the daughter later that day, she said, "Mom kept looking for you after you left."

On Wednesday, I was back. The daughter was feeding her mom. Again, Mom perked up when she heard music, and as I played several instrumental pieces, her attentiveness increased. The daughter mentioned that Mom was eighty-three and had been dealing with dementia for five years.

"Let me try a song that may seem a bit strange."

I began playing "Just Because," an old pop/blues/country tune that was written in the 1920s. It had been a huge hit in its time. The verse begins:

Just because you think you're so pretty,

Just because you think you're so hot,

and ends with:

I'm telling you, good gal,

I'm through with you,

Because, just because.

Along with the comic lyrics, the song has a catchy melody. By the time I got to the end of the first verse, Mom was smiling and tapping her toes.

Daughter had jumped to her feet and was shooting video on her cell phone. When I finished, she said, "Mom hasn't done a lot of smiling for the past several years. I definitely wanted to get a picture of that and the toe-tapping, for the rest of the family."

A surprising footnote: The following Tuesday, after finishing with our regular Tuesday night jam session, a couple who have been longtime jammers said, "I saw an interesting video of you this week. You were playing one of our favorite songs that you do." I wasn't aware of any recent video that might have been posted. Then they told me, "The video was on our next-door neighbor's phone. You played for her mom at the hospital. '*Just because you think you're so pretty…*'"

Sure enough, their next-door neighbors were the very same Mother and Daughter.

The world is big and blue and round,
Connections are made through sight and sound.
-JDM

"Brothers In Arms"

– DIRE STRAITS

A rock guitarist, a jazz pianist, and a Celtic fiddler walk into a room... I was there when it happened.

On a busy Thursday morning in the radiation lobby, the rock guitarist arrived first. We had a quick conversation before his follow-up appointment. As we were speaking, in strolled a well-known local jazz/classical piano player/professor. Not long after, a Celtic fiddler stepped through the door.

I thought, *If the four of us formed a group, we would certainly break some musical boundaries.*

Over the years, I've met tons of musicians. On another day, a professional blues guitarist borrowed my guitar to serenade his mother. Later, I made the same offer to a member of an Alice in Chains cover band. He declined. "My mom isn't wild about my music. It wouldn't go over well here."

If a guitarist appears knowledgeable and knows how to respect an instrument, I'll happily let him or her give my guitar a strum. The guy who tried to grab the Nightingale out of my hands didn't get that opportunity.

I've had great conversations with musicians of every stripe: church organists, bluegrass pickers, classical violinists, percussionists, and a professional French horn player. It's easy to connect; we're all a little weird in a similar way. Playing music has a way of re-wiring the brain. The proper term is cross lateralization of the hemispheres. But I digress.

Of all the musicians I've met in healing environments, the one who made the biggest impression on me was a saxophone player whose musical heyday was in the 1950s. We first met in the radiation lobby while his wife was going through treatment. He was a lively octogenarian. According to the calendar, he was in his mid-80s; but when it came to music, Chazz was in his mid-20s. One of the first things I liked about him was his ability to speak jazz without pretense. Terms like axe, cats, chops, dig, hip, in the pocket, jam, jive, woodshed, and many more were all part of his native language. If you can speak the language properly, you don't have to tell people you're part of the tribe.

Our times together usually began with some Brazilian jazz or a tune by Frank Sinatra. Chazz was an intent listener and always had encouraging things to say about my playing. Over the six weeks of his wife's treatment, he hipped me to the haps. Translation: He told me his story.

In his senior year of college at The Ohio State University, he had dropped out and headed to Florida. He and his trio were going to "make it big in the music business." Florida had a hot jazz scene, and he and his buddies were determined to be part of it.

Upon arriving in the Sunshine State, they were informed that a person couldn't work as a musician in Florida unless they had at least six months of residency. "It was a rule specifically created to keep out the likes of us!" he told me.

One fellow in the band found a job as a hotel bellboy and helped provide food and shelter for the group during this state of limbo.

While scoping the scene, they stumbled into a hot jam session where they hooked up with a bunch of heavy cats. Translation: They met some fellow jazz musicians at a musical gathering and became friends with several of the instrumentalists who were extremely talented at playing music spontaneously.

No doubt it was a hot jam session. One of the heavy cats was Cannonball Adderley, who later joined forces with Miles Davis.

During his time in Florida, Chazz met rockabilly guitarist Carl Perkins, one of the early pioneers of rock and roll. Carl invited Chazz to join his band. Chazz declined; he didn't want to break up the touring band he had put together.

Shortly after this, Carl almost died in a car accident as he was traveling to New York for an appearance on the Ed Sullivan Show. The show's crew had to scramble to find a replacement. They tracked down an up-and-comer who had a funny-sounding name and played in the same rockabilly style as Perkins. On the show, the kid covered a song Carl had written, "Blue Suede Shoes." The funny name was "Elvis," and the rest is history. Music, you are a fickle mistress.

Chazz told me plenty of tales from the road, and we had discussions about what it means to be a serious musician. Chazz was always very friendly and inclusive. "When we get through this (his wife's cancer treatment), we're going to have a party at the house. There will be lots of musicians. I hope you and your wife can make it."

Sadly, that day never came. When his wife passed away, I received a call from the family, inviting me to play music for her memorial service. It was a beautiful event, a tribute to a beloved mother and wife. Undoubtedly, any woman who can sustain a loving, 56-year marriage with a seriously dedicated musician is a saint.

The pastor who conducted the service was a Black man dressed in a cassock with a beautiful, multicolored stole. His gray-flecked hair was pulled back into a tight pigtail. His language was lyrical, his message melodic, free form fluent, happening, hypnotic.

Six months later, while playing in the hospital hallway, I heard a familiar voice. “Is that John Morgan out there?” It was Chazz, now in the middle of his own bout with cancer. He stepped out of his room with a nurse close behind holding his hospital gown shut. They were on the way to the shower room. I followed them, playing one of his favorites, “Fly Me to the Moon.” It was our own mini version of a New Orleans jazz march!

We got to the door of the shower room and I said, “This is as far as I go.” We laughed.

Fifteen minutes later, the nurse tracked me down. “Come with me,” she said. “Chazz is done with his shower and would like you to accompany him back to his room.”

When I arrived with the nurse, he was clean and smiling. He immediately began singing “The Girl from Ipanema.” I accompanied him again as we paraded back to his room, where our musical dialogue continued. He ended with, “When I get through this, we’re going to have a party at the house. I hope you and your wife will be able to make it.”

In the same way that music crosses cultural borders, it transcends age. Chazz was my senior by decades; even so, he treated me as a peer and co-conspirator in the plot to take over the world with music and goodwill.

Each generation brings their own sound to the fore; but at the core, musical hearts are much the same. Everyone is musical to some degree, but some of us get hit by the “music bug” at the genetic level.

When musicians meet, it's a
blessing and a treat.
Born to the same tribe, we
live the same vibe.
- JDM

9

"Getting Better"

— THE BEATLES

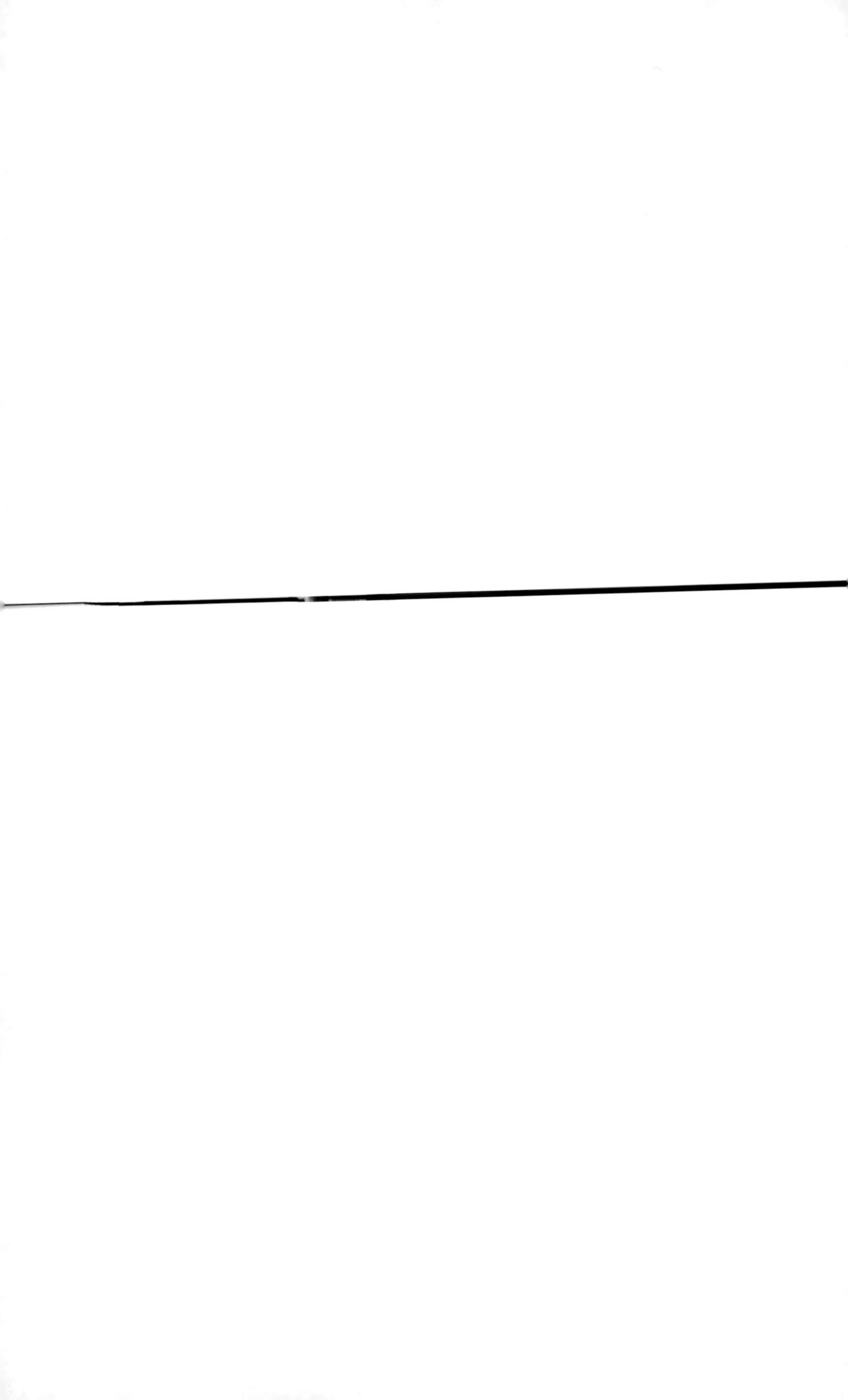

"Make Me Smile"

– CHICAGO

It had been a long day, three and a half hours of music in the infusion area and three hours on the cancer floor. I was walking across the atrium, headed toward the parking deck. Out of the corner of my eye, I noticed an attractive woman waving and walking in my direction. She was dressed in fashionable jeans and a stylish red sweater. She had a short, sassy haircut and a big smile.

"Hi, I just wanted to thank you for playing music for me when I was going through chemo."

Her smile looked familiar, but I think she could tell by my expression that I didn't quite recognize her. Trying not to come across as the completely absent-minded musician that I am, I said, "That was great. Do you remember what songs I played?"

"I sure do. You played three of my favorite worship songs." As she named the tunes, the picture began coming into focus.

A year before, I had sung with this woman twice. The last time I saw her, she was sitting in a wheelchair, hunched over, clutching her stomach, slowly rocking back and forth, trying not to show the pain. She was wearing a red bandana du-rag wrapped around her bare head, a baggy gray sweatshirt, and a pair of these-are-yard-work-only sweatpants. The only similarities to the woman in front of me now were her bright eyes and radiant smile.

She said, "During chemo, I was so tired. Sometimes in this process you get so worn down you can't do for yourself. That's why it means so much when someone comes along and is willing to do for you. When we sang together it was amazing. It truly lifted my spirit."

She went on to tell me that she had just come from her six-month follow-up appointment. Much to her relief, the news was tremendous. No sign of cancer!

The next time I saw her was six months later. Our schedules had somehow synchronized once again. This time, she was coming from her one-year follow-up. Another excellent report and a beaming smile.

This encounter took place after I had been working for the hospital for about ten years. Earlier in my artist-in-residence experience, I rarely saw patients more than once or twice. Meeting up with my smiling friend was a marker for me. All the time, money, and brainpower that had gone into cancer research over the preceding decades was bearing more and more fruit. Even in my small corner of cancer world, I could see the progress. Patients with a type of cancer that would have taken them off the map in earlier years were now friends I would repeatedly see over months or years. They were living longer, with an improved quality of life.

This reminded me of a friend and fellow jammer. He received his cancer diagnosis with the words *nine months to live* included. Because of advancing treatments, he was able to enjoy his family, children, and grandchildren for five more years.

The work is ongoing, but thanks to thousands of smart people doing millions of smart things, there are many significant reasons for hope and celebration!

"The Best Day of My Life"

– AMERICAN AUTHORS

It was Wednesday morning, and I was sitting on one of the rolling stools in the cul-de-sac area of the infusion center. This area has enough room for me to pull up a rolling stool, balance my tablet on my knee, and do a little singing.

After a few songs, a woman in the infusion bay to my right motioned me over. She had a familiar face, but during the previous months, we had only exchanged brief greetings.

I scooted over to her bay and she began: "Today is hopefully my last treatment. I want to thank you for all the music. Music means so much to me. I was part of my church's worship team until this cancer came along. As a matter of fact, ten years ago I was a student in one of those huge guitar-training classes that you organized."

Many years before, I had helped to start and run an eight-week music program that introduced hundreds of people to my favorite instrument. This lady had completed the beginner and intermediate levels of the program. She was delighted that the skills she developed had given her the foundation and confidence to begin playing music in public.

Our conversation continued lightheartedly. We laughed as we remembered some of the antics of the various instructors. Then, her tone turned serious as her thoughts came back to the present.

"You know, when they start telling you about what to expect during chemo, it's a lot of scary stuff, loss of energy, loss of hair, loss, loss, loss. Nobody says anything about the good stuff."

She continued quietly. "The first day of my treatment, I was terrified. I didn't know anyone here. I knew what to expect, but I didn't know what to expect, if you know what I mean. I wondered what the room would look like, if the nurses would be friendly, and if the sight of other cancer patients would be too depressing. On top of that, I was thinking way too much about the side effects.

"When I arrived, everyone seemed to know just what I needed. Jen [the art therapist] introduced herself, and we made this memory bracelet." She pointed to her wrist. "I haven't taken it off since that first day. Your guitar music was floating through the air, and these nurses..." Smiling, she lifted her hands in the air, "they are amazing. It was the best day of my life!"

Those heartfelt words caught me off guard, but I understood what she was saying. Her pre-treatment fears had been overwhelming but faded as she received what each person on staff had to offer. She saw other patients sitting comfortably in reclining chairs, reading, relaxing, or watching television while receiving chemo. From the warm greeting by the friendly tech to the attentive nurse who took time to understand her situation, nothing about the experience was scary.

I'm sure she had other *best days of her life*, like falling in love, beginning a family, playing music, and many enjoyable times with friends. But this *best day* was something special. Much thought and planning had gone into creating a warm, welcoming environment. She was being served by a knowledgeable team of caring professionals. The icing on the cake was art, music, and the availability of a full range of integrative services.

Interesting choice of words, *the best day of my life*. Her experience of being embraced and cared for had cast out thoughts of fear and dread. Yes, that's a best day.

"Johnny B. Goode"

– CHUCK BERRY

One evening, I received a text from the nurse manager of the cancer floor. A patient inquiring about music therapy had prompted the after-hours contact.

She asked if I would come to the floor first thing the next morning. My regular schedule would have taken me there early the next afternoon. I sensed an urgency in her request and adjusted my schedule. No problem, flexibility is what we do.

As I passed the nurses' station on my way to the patient's room, his nurse stopped me.

"He's blind," she whispered. "That's why he is wearing sunglasses."

When I entered the room, a man wearing a bright red Cleveland baseball hat and dark glasses was sitting up in bed. His wife was quietly seated in a chair at the foot of the bed.

He was a middle-aged fellow, tall, cheerful, and chatty. As soon as I sat down at the bedside, he began quizzing me. *Where are you from? How long have you been playing music? How did you get started playing at the hospital?* and more. It was like a friendly job interview. His ears were creating a mental picture that his eyes couldn't see.

Once he had a sufficient mental photograph, he asked for a song. Bluegrass and old-school country music was his preference. He quietly sang along on "Folsom Prison Blues" and Hank Williams's classic "Hey Good Lookin'."

There was a knock on the door, and in walked a doctor. That's my cue to leave. I always respect the patient's privacy and don't want to violate HIPAA regulations.

When he heard me shifting in my seat to leave, he asked me to stay. "I want to hear a couple more songs."

The doctor heard the patient ask me to stay, so he made sure the patient knew it would be a serious discussion about the details of his medical condition. "Do I have your permission to talk about your medical situation with these people (his wife and me) in the room?"

The patient consented, and in an unrushed manner, the doctor delivered some very difficult news. The cancer which had been treated a year ago had returned and spread. There were not a lot of options for a positive path forward.

The patient and his wife questioned the doctor at length, asking for every detail. She was taking notes, and he asked the same questions, with slight variations, over and over, committing the words to memory.

I am regularly called into a room after a serious prognosis is delivered, but this was the first time I witnessed this type of consultation. The doctor had a wonderful bedside manner. It was touching to see how gentle and patient his responses were to every inquiry even when the same question was asked for the fourth time. And before leaving, he asked, "Do you have any other questions?"

After the doctor left, without missing a beat, the patient picked up where we had left off. Now I realized why he had asked me to stay. The message delivered was not unexpected. He was ready for more music. Each of his requests were from the soundtrack of *O Brother, Where Art Thou*? To quote one line from that very quotable movie, "It's what they call that old-timey music." Again, he quietly sang along with "In the Jailhouse Now," "Big Rock Candy Mountain," and "I'll Fly Away."

Undaunted by the doctor's news, this music fan began to unfold his story.

The prior year, he had been treated for cancer at the Cleveland Clinic. "It was a really low time for me," he said. "They clearly explained there was a ninety-nine percent chance I wouldn't make it. A music therapist came to my room daily with her guitar and a tambourine. I was so weak I could barely pick up the tambourine. She would play slowly while I tried to keep the beat. During one session, she made a recording for me. She strummed "Johnny B. Goode" on the guitar and put my name into the song. I'm convinced that music saved my life. It brought me out of that low place."

It was moving to hear how much this experience meant to him. Obviously, he had received top-notch medical care, which certainly helped him get through that low time; but what stuck in his mind and heart was the music. A holistic musical connection works on so many levels. Moving the patient away from troubling thoughts by personalizing a well-loved tune was a stroke of musical magic.

After I had played for twenty minutes, he was beginning to tire. As I was leaving, he thanked me. "What a blessing to hear live music!"

When I came back to the same floor right after lunch, the patient had been discharged. It turns out, the only reason he had been in the hospital that morning was to find out the results of his tests. Thanks to the caring, watchful eye of the nurse manager, he was able to experience one more positive encounter with the healing power of music, and I was grateful to be part of it.

10

The Giving Gift

“My Back Pages”

– BOB DYLAN

It is Christmas Day, 1969. The living room is crowded, a Christmas tree in the corner, Mangee and Paupau (Grandmother and Grandfather) on the couch, Mom and Dad on the love seat, siblings Tom, Jane, and I perched on chairs and floor cushions.

All the obligatory gifts have been given, socks, underwear, new toothbrushes, and lime-scented English Leather cologne for the boys. At last, time to open the final gift, the one I’ve been dreaming about. In younger years, the final gift might have been a train set or BB gun. (“You’ll shoot your eye out!”) This year, I am a senior in high school. I have been playing music publicly for six years.

Please, please, let it be something musical.

It’s a rectangular package, about an inch thick. It feels like a book. Yes, yes, a large book. I tear away the wrapping, and it’s... *The Judy Collins Songbook.*

What the...! I am devastated. I’ve been part of this family all my life, and they don’t even know me. OK, it *is* a musical present, and Sweet Judy Blue Eyes is the inspiration for Crosby, Stills and Nash’s musical masterpiece “Suite: Judy Blue Eyes.” She sings like an angel and a ruby-throated sparrow. She’s one of the top two female folkies of this era. I love to listen to her music, but this is not *my* music. I play guy music; my guitar heroes are guys, guys like Jimi Hendrix, Eric

Clapton, the Beatles, the Rolling Stones, James Taylor, Neil Young, Crosby, Stills & Nash, not this girlie folk music.

Tom and Jane probably received nice presents, presents that make sense to them, but I am in a fog. My "big" Christmas present is an inch-thick book of songs I will never play. Oh, woe is me, the forever misunderstood artist.

As we clean up the wrapping paper and everyone is getting ready for brunch, Dad says, "Why don't you take a look at 'Both Sides Now'?"

Well, if I'm going to learn a Judy song, it might as well be one of her biggest hits.

I look in the index, turn to the page, and find a handwritten note with this enigmatic instruction: "Go look under your bed."

I look around the room. All eyes are on me.

Down the stairs to my basement bedroom I head. Under my bed, I find a handle, and the handle is attached to a guitar case, a Martin guitar case, and inside that case is a gorgeous Martin D-28, yes, with Brazilian rosewood sides and back. This is the real-deal, industry-standard, music-making machine. It's what my acoustic heroes play!

I quickly returned to the living room, in a state of emotional whiplash. My family may not understand me, but they do know me. I'm sure I played something, but who knows what it might have been.

As soon as the dishes are cleared from the table, I inconspicuously retreat to my basement lair and begin working on a fingerstyle version of "The First Noel." It's the first of my Christmas arrangements, a style that will become very important to me in a couple of decades when *Capture the Night* becomes my best-selling CD.

* * *

Later, I found out that my folks had paid the unbelievably extravagant, way-over-Christmas-budget price of $675 for this magnificent instrument. I don't think they ever understood their musically obsessed boy, but I do know they loved me. This over-the-top gift is just one expression of their love and support.

Oh, and the reason for a Judy Collins songbook: It was the only songbook of contemporary music available in the only music store of our little town.

This guitar was one of the most significant gifts I have ever received. It was instrumental in setting my life direction. Throughout my high school and college years, music opened doors to a wider world.

Playing live music is always a risky adventure. Even a small gig can gather an audience and set the stage for glory or humiliation. If the artist, primitive or professional, has something to offer—entertainment and something worthy of consideration—the audience will have something to give back—energy and appreciation.

This exchange is what gives music its power, the recognition of our shared humanity, a reminder of the pulse, melody, and harmony that dwells within.

My Christmas gift of 1969 was, and is, the instrument that showed me how to move what is in my heart through the open air to the ears of friends, family, and beyond. It is the gift that continues to give.

"Guitar Man"

– BREAD

I was playing quiet instrumental music at the north end of the hallway. A woman cautiously emerged from the last room on the right side of the hall and asked, "Could you come in and play some music for my boyfriend?"

"I would be happy to." This was my reason for being at the hospital, part of a normal day. But when I stepped into the room, normal flew out the window.

In the bed was Paul, perhaps the most enthusiastic guitar player/promoter I have ever known. It would take many words to accurately describe him. Some of those words would be *charismatic, energetic, unstoppable, a million-dollar smile,* and *always up for an adventure.* He was passionate about everything he found interesting in life, but his top-of-the list obsession was fingerstyle guitar, specifically, the Kentucky-born Merle Travis, Chet Atkins kind of pickin'.

Paul and I first met at one of his monthly Saturday afternoon pickin' parties. He would rent the community room of the Griswold Center in Worthington and turn it into an impressive music venue complete with a stage and a nice PA system. Everyone who came through the door was greeted and treated like an old friend. The delightful aroma of homemade soup filled the room. The cost of admission was a donation. For a few dollars more you could pick up a bowl of soup and a sandwich. The music got rolling at 1:00 when a bunch of pickers would circle the chairs and take turns playing their favorite Chet and Merle tunes. A little after 2:00, a special guest—often a hot picker from Nashville—would take the stage and the official concert would begin, no laser lights or fog machines, just great music. It was an amazing privilege to see topflight musicians in such an intimate setting.

Paul was responsible for two of my most memorable musical experiences. The first was a Saturday afternoon when he booked international guitar master Richard Smith as the special guest. Richard had been the featured performer at three previous parties. He always put on a sterling performance.

This time, unknown to Richard, Paul had a surprise up his sleeve. Never one to shy away from "mixing things up a bit," he had arranged for local violinist Arkadiy Gips to show up unannounced, violin in hand. By describing Arkadiy as a local musician, I simply mean that he lives in central Ohio. He was born in Kiev, Ukraine, and his musical resume is full of international performances and accolades, including an international tour with pop star Madonna.

Halfway through Richard's performance, Arkadiy walked in as arranged. Paul accompanied him to the stage and said, "Richard, I have someone I would like you to meet. This is Arkadiy. He plays the violin."

Richard, slightly nonplussed, looked skeptically at his new bandmate, a big man with bushy brown hair and full beard. The violinist unpacked his instrument. There was a brief moment of "What do you want to play?" "I dunno, what do you what to play?"

Richard hit a lick of "Sweet Georgia Brown." Arkadiy fired back with a matching lick plus embellishments. Richard threw down another red-hot riff, and Arkadiy answered with a musical touché.

Bang! After sizing each other up, they were off to the races! Two virtuosos going head-to-head in a joyful battle of musical wits. Each verse, each chorus poked, challenged, and tickled. Yes, music can tickle.

The crowd of assembled musicians was hooting and hollering like a Saturday night in the saloon. If this had been a bar fight, chairs and tables would have been flying and windows shattering. But it wasn't a battle. These musical gladiators, unknown to each other until five minutes ago, were smiling and laughing, pushing each other to higher heights of creativity. Just when it seemed like the room would explode from the intensity, the two titans brought "Sweet Georgia Brown" home for a graceful landing. The crowd was in a state of euphoria, backslapping and handshaking all around. We had just witnessed the pinnacle of what a live musical performance can be, a spontaneous and sublime moment that could never be repeated.

This is what Paul loved to do—bring together two musically combustible elements, mix them, and see what might happen. Would it be glory or gory? Paul, the musical chemist, knew how to make sure it was always glory.

The second most memorable event took place at a Tommy Emmanuel concert at the Riffe Center in downtown Columbus. Tommy is one of my absolute favorite guitarists. His live performances are astounding. I've seen him at least ten times, and each show is more astonishing than the one before.

On the way out of the theater, I saw Paul. We stopped to chat. After a little catching up, he leaned over with a conspiratorial twinkle in his eye and whispered, "You wanna meet Tommy?" There was only one answer to that question! Pointing, he said, "Meet me by that door in fifteen minutes. Don't go over there early. And act nonchalant."

Connie and I retreated to an inconspicuous place in the lobby and waited.

At the appointed time, we moseyed casually toward the secret door. There we met up with Paul and eighteen other Tommy fans. The door cracked open, and, without a word, we were ushered into a large conference room where we stood in a hushed circle.

Tommy's manager walked in through a door on the other side of the room. She explained, "Tommy is very tired. In a few minutes he will come in. He will say only 'Hello. Thank you,' then leave. Don't expect anything more."

A few minutes later, in walked the Man, the Legend. He said "Hello" but then proceeded around the circle, shaking hands and having a brief personal conversation with each person.

When he got to Paul, Paul said, "May I ask you a question?"

"Certainly."

"I have a guitar club here in town. Our motto is *A group of guitarists dedicated to preserving the music of Merle Travis and Chet Atkins*. Would it be okay if we added your name to that list?"

"I would be honored, Paul."

He continued around the circle, thanking each of us for coming. Then a wave goodbye, and he was gone.

As a funny side note, Paul wasn't always a Tommy fan. When Tommy, the Australian "wonder from down under," was breaking into the American guitar scene, Paul saw him as a Chet Atkins wannabe. He once commented to a fellow guitarist, "I wouldn't walk across the street to hear Tommy play."

Years later, Paul was a thoroughly converted fan and was sitting next to Tommy at a guitar convention in Nashville. At one point in the conversation, Tommy looked at him and said with a chuckle, "Paul, I didn't know you lived on this side of the block." The "wouldn't cross the street" comment had made the rounds in the close-knit finger-picking guitar community.

But now years had passed, and we were in a hospital room. With his million-dollar smile still intact, my friend Paul was sitting in a bed on the cancer floor. I knew what kind of music he enjoyed. I played a Chet-style tune. Then he requested one of my originals.

He thanked me and said, "John, things aren't looking too good for me. I appreciate you stopping by."

I don't normally do this without an invitation, but this was a friend I might never see again. I asked him if we could pray together. In typical Paul fashion, he replied, "It couldn't hurt."

Two weeks later, Facebook lit up with the news. Paul was gone. There were many fond remembrances. His unique life had an abiding impact on many people in and beyond the guitar community.

Rest well, dear friend, rest well.

"You've Got a Friend"

– JAMES TAYLOR

It was a Tuesday evening. Jam night! As soon as I walked into the main room of Java Central, Kerry, one of my fellow jammers, said, "I have something for you."

I'm thinking, *Very cool. He's loaning me a feedback buster* (a plastic sound hole cover). The week before, Kerry had asked if I ever used a feedback buster to help prevent feedback from my acoustic guitar when running it through a PA system. I had one on order, but it hadn't arrived yet.

Instead of pulling a round piece of plastic from his gig bag, Kerry quickly stepped over to the Java Central equipment closet, opened the door, and, with an excited grin, slowly turned, took three steps, and handed me a guitar case. "Sean wanted you to have this."

Sean had been a professional musician in New Orleans until Hurricane Katrina wiped out his jazz career and everything he owned. The city of Columbus was intended to be a short-term layover for him until the Big Easy was rebuilt, but life and love can override the best of plans. Columbus was now home.

Years earlier, Sean and I had occasionally crossed paths as part of the crew who hovered around Java Central, Ohio's best coffee shop and artistic hang out. Sean was also a committed mentor and encourager of young musicians. We didn't see each other often because gigging/teaching musicians are busy gigging and teaching.

Then one day at the hospital, Sean stepped into the hallway and invited me into a room to play for Sherry, his partner. They were two years into a difficult bout with an aggressive cancer. During this time, Sean had been working on a recording project, pulling together many of our mutual Java Central friends to help. Scheduling recording sessions around doctor appointments and chemo treatments made for a slow and difficult slog. During all of this, there was no gigging and only limited time for rehearsal. Perseverance paid off, and the project was finished shortly after Sherry's passing. In the shadow of that loss, there was no heart for putting together a marketing campaign. The project was enjoyed by friends and family.

Two years later, on a spring afternoon, I stood aside in the hallway as several patients, just out of surgery, were wheeled past. Instrumental music was flowing as I stood tight against the wall. As the last transport trolley rolled by, the patient, covered by a sheet and facing away from me said, “Why couldn’t they have played something like that during my procedure?”

A few minutes later, a lady approached me and asked, “Do you know Sean? He’s a regular at Java Central.”

“Sure!” I said, then realized that he was the person who had just rolled by.

It is always a privilege to bring musical comfort to anyone, even more so to a dedicated musical friend. Sean was a little groggy coming out of the anesthesia. Knowing that he was a James Taylor fan, I started with “Carolina in my Mind.”

He asked if I had ever met James Taylor. I laughed. “Yes, a couple of weeks ago. I was somewhere around the fiftieth row of Nationwide Arena, and James was on the stage.”

It turns out that Sean had met James at Tanglewood years before. “He’s very pleasant in person, but you can tell he has his own way of doing things. He’s very protective of his band and how they are treated.”

The grogginess was clearing up. “Blackbird” brought a smile, and “Here Comes the Sun” became a duet. The music and the conversation revived Sean and inspired a picture and a Facebook post declaring the playing and singing “revived my soul. I can’t wait to get home and finish setting up my music room.”

A few months later when we met again at the hospital, things were going the wrong direction. Sean was too tired to sing. Most of our time was spent catching up on the latest happenings at Java Central. A week later I was back, and Sean was sleeping. No music, no conversation. It wasn’t long till I learned that he was in hospice.

I was on call, in case there was an appropriate time for a visit. That time never came.

Back at the coffee shop, I placed the guitar case Kerry had handed me on a bench in front of me. The travel case had a Seagull logo on the front. Seagull guitars are well-made Canadian instruments with solid wood tops and a reasonable price. The only Seagulls I had played were entry level, so I wasn't sure what to expect.

When I unzipped the case, Bam! I recognized this instrument at once. It was a limited-edition Taylor. It was part of a special series of guitars that had been released in October of 1997. There had been an extensive write-up in *Wood and Steel,* Taylor's promo magazine.

These guitars were movie stars. Their bodies were made of flamed black walnut from a 100-year-old tree that appeared in two movies, *Cujo,* based on a novel by Stephen King, and *Peggy Sue Got Married*, a time-travel romantic comedy. The instrument in front of me was a Cujo 14, number 59 of the 125 Grand Auditorium models made from that tree. The fretboard was intricately inlaid with key images from the Cujo movie: a full moon, a bat, the tree, and Cujo, the St. Bernard. The label was signed by Bob Taylor and Stephen King.

The guitar wasn't just a beauty to behold; it sang with a resonant cedar voice, sparkling highs, and punchy lows. Sean had recently had the instrument set up and restrung. It sounded and played like a dream.

Kerry told me that Sean had five excellent guitars that he designated to go to specific people. He had given Kerry a gorgeous electric 12-string. "But," Kerry said, "Cujo is the gem."

Later, when I saw a nurse navigator, a mutual friend of Sean's, I told her the story. "Yep," she said, "that's typical Sean! His generosity is a big part of who he was."

I knew this wasn't just a generous gift. This was a trust. Sean was all too familiar with my work at the hospital, which is exactly where Cujo and I went the next day, straight to the cancer floor.

On Wednesday morning, Cujo was proclaiming in the halls and rooms, *Celebrate the day, my friends, celebrate the day. The past is gone, the future awaits. Celebrate the day.*

Every earthy treasure
will soon be left behind.
Make generosity a legacy,
new treasures you will find.
– JDM

11

"My Little Town"

— SIMON & GARFUNKEL

"My Little Town"

– PAUL SIMON

I grew up during the 1960s in Gallipolis, "the Old French City," a small river town on the banks of the Ohio River. Like most small towns, it was full of characters. Ol' John, the night watchman, faithfully checked the downtown store locks every night. Another kind of watchman showed up in front of G. C. Murphy's Five and Dime on Saturday mornings and asked, "Wanna buy a watch?" Foxy, the world's coolest custodian, was always impeccably dressed, looked like Chuck Berry, and drove a Cadillac convertible.

Although Columbus is a two-and-a-half-hour drive from Gallipolis, several people made the trek from my hometown for specialized cancer treatment. One day I met the mother of a girl I had dated in high school. This lady was a local legend, thanks to her side business of making homemade pies. I also met the nephew of my tenth-grade algebra teacher and later was completely surprised to see a high school buddy who came from Washington, D.C., to spend time with his sister during her treatment. A few months later, I happened upon my second cousin, the son of a legendary restaurateur. He was tending to his mother. "Hey, Mom! Look who I found in the hallway!"

But perhaps the most convoluted small-town-life intersection occurred on what, to that point, had been a normal Wednesday.

I was playing quietly in the hall when a woman invited me into a room where her husband was resting in the bed. She told me he enjoyed music but was heavily sedated, going in and out of sleep. During this visit, he would pop up, and the three of us would talk briefly, I would play a song, and he would quickly drift off. A few minutes later, we would repeat the same sequence.

During one of the lulls, she mentioned that they lived in a small town south of Columbus. I told her that I grew up in southeast Ohio.

"Where?" she asked.

"Gallipolis."

"Have you ever heard of Remo's hot dog stand?"

That was like asking a person who grew up in Paris if they had ever heard of the Eiffel Tower. Remo's, also known as Rocchi's but officially named The Topsy Turvy, is an institution. From seventh through ninth grades, my buddies and I would race across a parking lot and through a muddy, gravel-filled alley to get to Remo's during our too-short lunch break. For 48 cents, a person could score a foot-long hot dog and a bottle of pop. The sauce is legendary. The recipe is a closely held family secret.

She asked if I knew that Remo had been in World War II. Gallipolis is a small town; I knew he was a veteran, but not much more. Since her husband was now soundly asleep, she went on with a story about her dad. Her father and Remo had been in the army, part of the 104th Infantry Division known as the Timber Wolves. While they were engaged in a battle, Remo was seriously injured. They were under heavy fire and preparing to retreat. Some of the men said, "Leave him. He's too far gone." Her dad, nicknamed Mike because of his last name, Carmichael, couldn't do that, "I can't leave him. He's my buddy."

Fortunately, Remo was a skinny young guy and Mike was a beefy football player. He threw Remo over his shoulder, carried him to a medical station, and returned to the fight. Mike was also seriously injured during the same battle and sent to England to recuperate. He never knew what happened to his buddy Remo.

Decades later they found each other. Now with careers and grown families, they both lived in southeast Ohio, about an hour apart. A few years after their reunion, the Gallipolis Chamber of Commerce asked Remo to be the Grand Marshall of the Veterans Day parade. He agreed but only on the condition that Mike would be the Co-Grand Marshall. “He’s the only reason I’m here.”

At the end of the parade, both families were together, Remo with his wife and children; Mike, now on oxygen and in failing health, with his wife and children, including the daughter who was telling me this story. The reunion was a time of tears, laughter, and deep appreciation for the risk Mike had taken, a risk that had and continues to have a far-reaching impact.

Remo’s, now run by one of his sons, is woven into the fabric of this beautiful river town. Multiple generations of fans wouldn’t think of passing through Gallipolis at lunchtime without dropping in.

Without Mike’s heroic action, an important part of this small-town culture would be missing, and no one would even know it. That is the power of one life.

When her husband awoke there was one more song, then on down the hallway.

"Shower the People"

– JAMES TAYLOR

There is nothing good about cancer. The day of a cancer diagnosis is the day your world turns upside down. It's the beginning of a battle. Thankfully, it's not the day you disappear from the map. It comes with a small mercy, the gift of time.

In the mid-60s, Bob Dylan plugged in his electric guitar, a radical action which grew into a new musical genre, folk rock. Folkie troubadours gave way to singer-songwriters. Folkie trios were replaced by acoustic rock bands. The Byrds, Buffalo Springfield, Poco, and Crosby, Stills and Nash blended their acoustic and electric guitars while James Taylor, Joni Mitchell, Cat Stevens, and Carly Simon amped up their folk ballads.

Tapping into this new vibe, my best friends and bandmates, Mark and Steve, traded their electric guitars for acoustics. We then joined forces with two lovely and talented ladies, Lisa and Paula. I don't think we ever got far enough to come up with a group name, but all of us sang and played guitar. There is no recorded evidence to the contrary, so allow me to say that we sounded just like all the artists mentioned above—at least, teenaged versions of those artists. We worked up a few of the top hits of the day and somehow managed to get a gig at a local college coffeehouse.

In my mind, a gig at a college coffeehouse surely signaled a huge break for our musical career. After all, people who played in coffeehouses got discovered, which led directly to recording contracts, tons of adoring fans, and, of course, the lavish lifestyle that folkies love to decry. Never mind that *those* coffeehouses were in New York and Los Angeles.

"Music career!" What world was I living in? This coffeehouse was indeed a house, the kind of cozy, white-picket-fence house you might find on the edge of a small college campus in southeastern Ohio. This house had recently come into the possession of Rio Grande College, now known as The University of Rio Grande. Regarding the "coffee" part of coffeehouse, yes, it was a place for students to hang out while enjoying coffee, snacks, and occasional live music.

The audience on the night of our gig was never more than ten people, including five of us in the band. Students were coming and going randomly, casually snacking and visiting with friends. There was no more chance of us being "discovered" than there was of a catfish hopping out of Raccoon Creek and walking two miles to hear us play.

At one point in the evening, I did a solo, one of my original songs. As I was playing, Paula and Lisa, sitting behind me, were talking and giggling. I was singing and simmering. Didn't they know this was our—*my*—opportunity to make it to the big time? How could they not be totally enthralled by this mind-blowing song which was sure to be playing on radios across the country in a matter of months? When I finished, I turned and said, "Paula, you really piss me off!"

Yes, it was rude, crude, and totally uncalled for, but such is the mind of a self-absorbed teenage boy. James Taylor hadn't yet sung, *"What you plan to do with your foolish pride when you're all by yourself alone?"*

Fortunately, no serious relational damage was done, though my rash comment came back to haunt me as the punch line to many of my own goofy missteps: "John, you really..."

Decades later, it occurred to me: You and I will only interact with a tiny fraction of the seven billion people living on earth. The number of people who will have a meaningful, positive impact on our lives is even smaller. Wouldn't it be wise to treat those teachers, preachers, friends, and family as the miraculous gifts they truly are? As James Taylor would later write, *"Shower the people you love with love."*

There is nothing good about cancer, but it doesn't arrive as the sudden flash of a car crash or a 3:00 am phone call from an emergency room.

What can be accomplished with the small mercy of time?

We pray for the healing of bodies broken,
but there's a deeper healing in what can be spoken.
- JDM

12

"More to This Life"

— STEVEN CURTIS CHAPMAN

"Heart of Gold"

– NEIL YOUNG

I settled into the cul-de-sac at the far end of the infusion suite and began playing a few songs. A woman pushing her chemo pole walked past me on the way to the restroom. She quietly whispered, "Neil Young, 'Heart of Gold.'" I finished the song I was playing and knocked out the intro riff to Neil's 1972 classic.

About fifteen minutes earlier, I had heard a nurse getting a patient settled into one of the nearby infusion bays. Though I couldn't hear the conversation, I heard plenty of hearty laughter from that direction. The nurse and this first-time patient were getting to know each other.

When I finished "Heart of Gold," a voice from the nearby bay called out, "You sound just like Neil Young!"

I turned to see a young Black woman sitting in the infusion chair. At my age, I can call most of the population "young," so allow me to clarify: This young lady appeared to be around forty, but from what she later told me, she was closer to my age. Her name was Junie.

I rolled my stool over to her and said, "Wait a minute. You are way too young to even know who Neil Young is!"

With a quick laugh and a glance at my hospital badge, she replied, "John, I'm older than you think." Picking up on her jovial attitude, I decided to push it a bit.

"That may be, but you still aren't old enough to know about Neil. I'll bet you tell every old white guy with a guitar slung over his shoulder, 'You sound just like Neil Young.'"

She really cackled on that one and replied, "Listen, I know Neil, James Taylor, Crosby, Stills and Nash, Carly Simon, Joni Mitchell, and Carol King too."

This really caught me off guard.

"Okay," I said, "explain this to me: Why don't you like Motown?"

"Oh, Motown is all right. That's what all my friends listened to when I was growing up."

At that point, Junie's sister walked into the bay. I said, "We were just talking about music." Her sister rolled her eyes and said, "Yep, she's crazy!" More laughter all around.

Junie, my surprising folky fan, continued unwinding her musical history. It all started when she cozied up to the radio as a little girl and heard the warmth of James Taylor's voice and the beautiful harmonies of Crosby, Stills and Nash. She would listen to the radio on the way to school and fall asleep to the gentle voices at night.

When she tried to introduce this music to her friends they would say, "Girl, you're crazy! What are you doing, listening to that stuff?" Back in the day when vinyl was state-of-the-art, she bought albums. When she showed her friends the artists on the covers, they would shake their heads in disbelief. "How can you like those hairy people?" But like them she did, unapologetically.

I was able to play for Junie a half dozen times. Her requests always included some Neil Young, "Old Man" or "Heart of Gold," some James Taylor, "Up on the Roof" or "You've Got a Friend," and "Our House" by Crosby, Stills and Nash.

Interestingly, we found crossover points between Motown and folk music. I would bring up "How Sweet It Is to Be Loved by You." She thought of it as a James Taylor song, but I also remembered it as a 1964 hit by Marvin Gaye. The same with Sam Cooke's 1960 hit, "What a Wonderful World." In 1978, James Taylor teamed up with Simon and Garfunkel to cover that gem, but it's still Sam's song.

Junie had an excellent support system. Every week she was accompanied by her mother, sister, or daughter. They all shared the same great sense of humor, but Junie had the best and most infectious laugh.

One day when her sister stepped out of the bay, Junie began expressing how difficult it was to cope with cancer and the ongoing treatment. "I don't feel so good a lot of the time." It wasn't really a complaint, just a statement of fact: This is what my life's like now. She went on to say how the music took her mind off her circumstances. When her sister returned, she was back to her usual cheerful self. Laughter was her native tongue, but laughter didn't mean that everything was fine. It meant *I will choose to be happy regardless of what is going on*. Her words reminded me of Nightbirde (Jane Marczewski), another sister in the battle, who said. "You can't wait until life isn't hard anymore before you decide to be happy."

The lessons I learned from my times with Junie were far deeper than "Don't judge a book by its cover." Junie was complex. She was a model of living on her own terms in the positive present. Her laughter said, "I will enjoy the music I want to enjoy; I will love the people God puts in my life; and I will choose to be joyful even in the face of adversity."

One of the last times I saw Junie, she told me with a wink, "There's more to this life than what we see."

"What a Wonderful World"

– LOUIS ARMSTRONG

In hundreds of conversations with patients, I've asked, "Is there an artist or style of music that you enjoy?" Many times, the answer has been, "Oh, I like everything." With a little more questioning, I've discovered this actually means, "I like everything that I like."

One Thursday afternoon, I sat down with a gentleman in the infusion area. When I asked what music he would enjoy, he said, "I really like Pentatonix; they have such great harmonies. Have you heard of them? They're fantastic, and I love everything they've done. I also like show tunes. *Oliver* has so many great songs, and of course, there is *Les Misérables*. I also like James Taylor, Jim Croce, and John Denver. If you are talking female folkies, you can't beat Joni Mitchell and Judy Collins, and I also like Peter, Paul, and Mary, but if you want to talk about blues, it's Bonnie Raitt and B.B. King. Did you know B.B. and Eric Clapton did an album together? It's fantastic! And don't forget Muddy Waters and Motown. I grew up on Motown. Of course, I always try to listen to some classical music every day; the London Symphony, wow..."

This went on for about five minutes. Here was a guy who had the broadest musical range of anyone I had ever met in the hospital.

He was receiving infusion treatment for a disease that wasn't cancer, but it was something that kept him close to home, always close to a toilet. "The only time I go out is to come here for treatment. My niece goes to the store for me." As we talked, he told me that he lived alone. A few relatives checked in on him, but he didn't like to trouble them. He told me he spent at least eight hours a day on the internet, exploring every kind of music that caught his attention.

I decided to test a theory I have. "Do you get along with a lot of different types of people?" I asked.

He thought for a moment, "Well, now that you mention it, before I got sick, I had a lot of friends from widely differing backgrounds."

"Let me run this idea by you," I said. "It seems to me that musical styles represent approaches to life, ways of thinking, so to speak. It's as though each style is a compilation of values that are communicated lyrically and musically. People are attracted to the style or styles of music that best represent their beliefs. A musical style can be a means of philosophical shorthand. Back when vinyl ruled the musical world, I remember going to friends' houses and checking out their 'cool factor' by perusing their record collection." We both laughed.

"We could say rock and roll means 'Let's party.' Traditional folk music tells stories. Country music does much the same, with the addition of steel guitars and fiddles. Singer-songwriter music tends to be more introspective, like a page from someone's journal. Bluegrass is traditional and conservative. Celtic is much like bluegrass with additional Irish hijinks. Classical music appeals to the desire for complexity within structure. Jazz is complexity with spontaneity.

"Here's where I'm going with this," I continued, "no one is limited to the number of styles they're allowed to enjoy, but people who embrace a wider range of musical styles seem to find it easier to get along with more kinds of people."

He looked at me thoughtfully. "You know, you may be on to something. I really love people, all kinds of people, and I really love music. I just plain love life, everything about it. I love life so much; I can't imagine myself not being part of it."

That last spontaneous statement, punctuated by his tears, was so deep and personal, it shattered me. His connection to music and life were one and the same.

I have pondered this man's statement for years, along with something my eighty-six-year-old father said to me shortly before he passed: "It all went by so fast."

In this handsbreadth of time that we call life, do I actively appreciate the variety of people who surround me? Do I listen to their music? Do I listen to them?

I try to remind myself daily to appreciate the skills, the talents, the *joie de vivre* of those people who surround me. Actively appreciating these folks has helped me understand my place on the map.

"This Little Light of Mine"

– CHILDREN'S TRADITIONAL SONG

I was invited into a room at the far end of the cancer floor. In the bed was a middle-aged Black woman. She was surrounded by friends, two couples plus two ladies. Each person was stylishly dressed, the men in suits, the ladies in tastefully elegant dresses. I would realize later that this was a sign of respect for their dear friend.

The patient was smiling and didn't show any outward signs of illness. I had played for folks in the hospital long enough to know outward appearances cannot be trusted. There were clues: She was attached to an infusion line, and the conversation in the room indicated these visitors had traveled a long distance to see her. They were from "back home."

I introduced myself and asked the patient if she had any favorite songs. Having spotted the Gideon Bible on the tray table, I wasn't surprised when she asked for "Jesus Loves Me" followed by "This Little Light of Mine." When I finished, there were misty eyes in the room. One of the men asked if I knew "Amazing Grace."

"Sure. I don't mind singing by myself, but if you are so inclined, it would be even better if we could sing together."

I extend this invitation regularly, but in this case, I was acting on a bit of intuition. I was in a room with folks who were dressed for Sunday morning. There had to be three or four excellent singers in a gathering like this. Yes, two words later, when we all hit "grace" I knew I was in the middle of the choir. Strong melodies, lush harmonies, raised hands. We were in church.

Worship in the hospital room of a patient in critical condition is different than Sunday morning worship. The love and intimacy in this room was tangible. We moved into "How Great Thou Art." Eyes closed, hands in the air, the choir was fully engaged.

When we finished, one of the gentlemen walked with me into the hallway. He thanked me, shook my hand, and held it.

"I have a word for you," he began. "God is using you and will continue to use you in a very prophetic way to touch and heal people." He continued with more words of encouragement regarding my involvement with music and healing, and he ended with a short prayer and blessing.

It turned out that he and the other man in the room were pastors from Alpharetta, Georgia. These folks had come to spend time and share memories with their dear friend.

This was early in my experience at the hospital. I had begun as a guitar player looking for a gig. This journey was turning into something much more than that. This man's words of prophetic encouragement have resonated in my soul, continually reminding me why I'm here. Even now, writing this twenty years later brings me to tears, thinking of God's goodness and mercy. We humans are like broken clay pots, but it's that brokenness that lets our little light shine through.

"Amazing Grace"

– JOHN NEWTON

On a Monday afternoon, I was playing an upbeat variation of "Wildwood Flower" when a guy and gal walked by. They appeared to be in their early thirties and were nicely dressed in what I would call country casual.

He stopped and looked at the headstock of my guitar, a good sign that he was a guitar picker. She continued down the hall. He was familiar with Ryan guitars.

"That thing sounds great. Tell me about it," he said.

I gave him a tour of the incredible craftsmanship and innovation that contributed to this instrument's amazing voice. It was obvious he knew a lot about music and guitars.

"What do you play?" I asked.

"I'm not much of a picker, but I'm a backup singer in Nashville, so I do know a lot of pickers."

Our conversation continued in that direction for a few minutes, then he said, "I've got to get back to Dad's room. Could you stop there in about fifteen minutes?"

When I arrived, the man in the bed was a big fellow, tall and sturdily built, but he was unresponsive, eyes closed. Six or seven young adults of about the same age as the fellow I had spoken with surrounded his bed.

"What would your dad like to hear?"

The singer replied, "Do you know 'Amazing Grace'?"

I strummed the first chord and began, "A-a-h..."

On "-mazing," the room exploded, the walls evaporated, the ceiling flew away, and I was floating in a river of multicolored, crystalline harmony. It was the vocal equivalent of a perfectly tuned, 12-string guitar, rich and resonate. Transcendent. The voices surrounding the father were singing in four-part harmony, and a quick glance around the room revealed eyes closed and moist.

The sound was tangible, so beautiful I had to remind myself to keep playing. The only thing running through my head was, *Don't mess this up, don't mess this up.*

Without a word, we floated from "Amazing Grace" to "In the Garden" to "It is Well With My Soul" to "How Great Thou Art." As the last note faded, the Nashville singer gave me a thumbs up and mouthed the words "thank you." I quietly slipped out of the room and back into the hum of hospital activities.

In a lifetime of playing and listening to music, I had never experienced anything like this. To say the sound was multicolored and crystalline is simply to report what my closed eyes saw. For a moment, the separation between heaven and earth was very thin. It was as though the dividing curtain between time and eternity had been drawn back. Whatever happened, my mind and heart had been washed by something pure and clean. It was a transforming blend of light and love that stayed with me for the next three days.

When I saw my Nashville friend in the hallway later that afternoon, I said, "Dude, *what was that*?"

He laughed. "Dad is a retired Quaker pastor. Those are my sisters, cousins, and their spouses. As kids, we accompanied Dad to his speaking engagements, and he always included us in the service. We would sing several hymns before his message. We've sung together for decades, but now we all live farther apart, so we don't get together as much as we would like."

I thanked him for inviting me into that experience. "You're welcome," he smiled.

If hearing is the last sense a person loses before death, I can only imagine what was going on in that retired pastor's mind as he heard these beloved children singing his favorite songs.

Have I been to heaven? No, but I've stood on the doorstep and listened.

"Spirit in the Sky"

– NORMAN GREENBAUM

Every day our immune system constantly protects us from millions of harmful invaders, viruses, bacteria, and mutated cells. It fights to protect us, and it also assists in healing. As amazing as the human immune system is, cancer can sometimes evade, overwhelm, and even hijack it to assist the rogue cells in their attack upon the body. The ability of cancer to mutate in response to chemotherapy and other factors makes this disease seem like a scheming, malicious foe on a suicidal mission.

Cancer feels like a personal enemy. It's not surprising that we use military language to discuss it: There is a war on cancer; it invades, attacks, occupies, and metastasizes (spreads) to other organs in the body.

If this is a battle, the patient is the frontline soldier. One line of thinking can be, if the battle isn't going well, maybe the soldier isn't doing enough to win the fight. This is a needless and unjustified burden for anyone already battling this brutal disease.

I agree that dealing with cancer is a battle, but I think we should reframe the fight. We live in a beautiful, broken world. Bad things happen to good people, and bad people sometimes seem to skip through life unscathed. I think the actual battle has to do with how well we live rather than how long we live. The truth is, we are all on a one-way street that eventually comes to an end. Whether the journey is long or short, victory is won by making the most of the time we are given. People who live a life of care and connection win the war.

I remember being called to a hospital room where a young woman, twenty-one years old, was sitting up in bed, talking with her parents and a friend. She was a picture of what anyone would hope for in a daughter: smart, cute, funny, musical, a National Honor Society student. She had just withdrawn from her freshman year at a prestigious university due to a very serious cancer diagnosis.

When I sat down, she asked for a couple of pop songs. After the music, she began talking to her parents and friend.

"I'll miss you, but I'm not afraid of dying. I know it doesn't all end here. I'll see you again." She went on to share that her faith assured her that life on this earth is only a beginning.

There were no dry eyes in the room that day. Then she asked for "Amazing Grace." Joy and sorrow can be wrapped in the same package.

I understood her reason for faith and hope. When I was in college, friends shared the same hope with me. They explained that God is personal, alive, and that He has revealed Himself through Jesus Christ. This stood in stark contrast to the hodge-podge belief system I had cobbled together. At that point, I was hoping to spend eternity as a continuously vibrating column of crystal-clear blue light and sound, surrounded by an infinite ocean of similar clear and colorful lights all pulsating in harmony. My imagery of eternity was a combination of cobbled together Eastern mysticism and the pristine sound that my flute professor had produced at my first lesson.

Although a glorious heaven with a loving God seemed the better option, I resisted. It took another year of observing how my Christian friends lived and treated one another, a reading of C.S. Lewis's *Mere*

Christianity, and an actual dive into the Bible to understand what this "personal, living God" stuff was all about. Strangely, I had considered myself an expert on the Bible without having ever seriously read it. Like many people, I had grown up with enough well-intentioned religious training to be immunized from the power of the Gospel.

Looking back, I can honestly say that I could never do what I have done without the assurance that there is a loving heavenly Father guiding my steps and wooing all of humanity to Himself. I have been at the bedside of many people whose faith has sustained them through their darkest of hours. I have seen families comfort and encourage one another in the face of great loss, knowing that in this life, the end is not the end.

13

“Try to Remember”

— THE BROTHERS FOUR

“Sing a Song”

– THE CARPENTERS

One Wednesday in the late afternoon, a nurse said, “You may want to stop in over there.” She pointed to a room near the south nurses’ station.

I knocked on the door and stepped in. A middle-aged woman was sitting up in bed, legs crossed under the covers. Three Gideon Bibles lay on the tray table extending across the bed, and the woman had another copy in her hands. She was staring intently at the cover. My first thought was, *Looks like I’ll be playing “Amazing Grace” in this room.*

She asked, “Can you do me a favor?”

“Sure, I’ll try.”

She pointed to the cover of the Bible in her hands. “Would you check to see if that is spelled correctly?”

I looked. “H-o-l-y-B-i-b-l-e. Yes, it looks good to me.”

“Thanks.”

Even though I had a clue, I asked what type of music she would enjoy.

“Oh, anything,” was her cheery response.

“How about ‘Amazing Grace’?”

“Oh yes, I like that one!”

I began, but before we got to "how sweet the sound," she stopped me and asked, "Could we do something different? I can't remember the words."

"Sure, what would you like?"

"Oh, anything. Could we just make something up?"

"Sure, not a problem."

I began slowly playing a basic chord progression in the key of G. She had a good sense of pitch and a pleasant voice. She began quietly humming a simple melody. Next came a few words, a combination of short phrases. "I love You, God. Thank you. You are my friend."

After about a minute, she stopped singing and asked, "Can we do another one?"

"Sure." Still in the same key but with a different chord progression and rhythm, she came up with another flowing tune. "Jesus, I love You, thank you for loving me. You are so good."

Her voice gently filled the room, then she stopped.

"That was fun. Can we do it again?"

And so the process continued. After five songs, her nurse came in to see how things were going. "Listen to this," I said. Two more short songs were sung into existence.

After the nurse left, this sweet songbird looked at me and said, "Do you know what kind of cancer I have?"

"No."

"It's brain cancer. I don't feel bad but sometimes I do funny things. Let me know if I do something funny. Can we do another song?"

"Sure."

"On the Road Again"

– WILLIE NELSON

Music reaches beyond the intellect into unseen places and unearths buried treasure.

One day after I finished up my afternoon on the cancer floor, I passed through the lobby of the treatment center located across the street from the main hospital. A woman was sitting on a bench next to the concierge, waiting for a cab.

"What's in the case?" she asked.

I looked at the big, blue, carbon-fiber container hanging from my shoulder and gave her a quick smile. "You'll never believe it; it's a guitar."

"Well then, are you going to play me a song?"

It was the end of the day, and there was nothing on my schedule till dinner in about an hour and a half. I sat down next to her on the bench.

"What's your favorite type of music?"

"Oh, anything. What kind of music do you play?"

"Well, there's country or rock or some old jazz, but a lot of folks like James Taylor."

Her eyes lit up. "Oh yes, James Taylor. Do something by him."

"Carolina in my Mind" is a good opener. It conveys a sense of longing for home that connects with folks.

Her face grew serious. Her attention was laser focused as she joined in on the first verse and sang all the lyrics with me. We went straight into another JT song, "Shower the People," a powerful expression of intentionally loving the people in your life.

There are people who sing, and there are people who SING. Even in this casual setting, this lady was all in. Her singing came from a deeply emotional place. She conveyed not just words but also a profound connection with the song that is rare and beautiful. She was a living example of what it means to sing from your heart.

I asked, "Do you like Willie Nelson?"

"Oh yes, do something by Willie Nelson."

We were immediately "On the Road Again."

She was in from word one and never missed a line. We were halfway through another song when her cab arrived. She thanked me and expressed how much she had enjoyed singing together.

After she left, Kathy, the concierge, stared at me with a look of astonishment. "That was amazing!"

"Yes," I said, "she has a wonderful voice."

"Not that," she laughed. "She comes here regularly, and I've assisted her many times. She has serious brain and memory issues. Before you got here, she asked for a drink of water. When I brought her a cup, she sat there with it in her hands for several minutes, then said, 'I forgot what I'm supposed to do with this. Do you know?' The fact that she remembered all those songs was a miracle."

The human brain is one of the most amazing marvels on Earth. Even when damaged or malfunctioning, it can still accomplish the seemingly miraculous. Music can awaken sleepy neurological pathways that have lain dormant for decades. How does that happen?

I'll leave the explanation to science. In the meantime, I'm happy to witness the wonder.

"Tapestry"

– CAROL KING

One day while I was unpacking my guitar in the nurse's break room, I overhead a conversation. Two of the nurses were talking about what it's like when patients behave in abnormal and aggressive ways. Knowing that I sometimes get called into abnormal and aggressive situations, I asked them what was going on.

First, they spoke generally about brain cancer patients who often act in ways that are completely out of character. The gentle grandmother who begins cussing like a sailor, the kindly gentleman who becomes crude and abusive to his family and caregivers.

"As a matter of fact, we have a man right now who is driving us and his wife crazy. He's extremely demanding and impatient. It's very hard on his wife. She keeps telling us, 'This isn't him. This isn't him! He doesn't act like this.'"

When I arrived at my usual location at the far end of the hall, I noticed a room that was getting a lot of in and out traffic of nurses and techs. When I moved down the hall, just a few feet from this room, I heard a bed alarm go off. This was followed by the sound of shuffling feet and the bumping sound of furniture being moved. Before I got to the door, a tech arrived and gently taking the patient by the hand said, "You've got to get back in bed. You need to stay in bed."

"No, let me go out there! I want to see where the music's coming from!"

Aha, now I knew which room the nurses had been talking about.

I stepped into the doorway. "How about if I come in and play a little music for you?"

The tech carefully got him back into bed, covered up and settled. I pulled up a chair. "What kind of music do you enjoy?"

He was an old-school country fan. We started off with Johnny Cash, then went on to Willie Nelson. In place of restless agitation there was now smiling, singing, and foot-tapping under the covers. We had pleasant conversations between songs. He told me what he liked about the songs and the singers. "Now, Johnny and Willie, they are American legends." It was a warm, friendly interaction with a true fan.

After a few songs, his wife came into the room. Her face was tense. She had the look of a person whose nerves are frazzled, unsure of what might happen next.

As she tuned in to the conversation, her expression changed. Her face relaxed and slowly broke into a faint smile. Her husband of more than five decades was talking like the kind-hearted man she knew and loved. The conversation moved to hymns. We sang "In the Garden" and "Amazing Grace," and he told me how much these songs had meant to him throughout his life.

When I left the room, his wife followed me into the hall.

"Thank you so much. He has always been a great music lover, and that is the calmest he has been in days."

As I turned to go, a nurse immediately approached me and asked if I could stop by a room and play some music for an elderly lady with dementia. I popped in and introduced myself. The lady was sitting in the bed with a cafeteria menu on her lap. We had a nice conversation, albeit with several illogical rabbit trails.

When I asked her what she would like to hear, she replied, "Just the usual stuff."

From our conversation, I knew she liked folk music. As I played "You are My Sunshine" and "Country Roads," she stared fixedly at the menu as if it were a lyric sheet. Occasionally she sang a line or two, then a smile, thanks, and goodbye.

That evening at dinner, Connie and I were talking about my encounter with the agitated gentleman. We were once again amazed at the way music brought calm to such a stress-filled situation. As we were discussing this, the phone rang.

The caller ID lit up with the name of a woman I hadn't spoken to in over ten years. The last time we had been in touch, she was working at a Christian school and coordinating a mercy mission, raising money for one of the families whose children attended the school. The father of this family had been tragically injured in a motorcycle accident. Why hadn't I run into Nicole during the past ten years? She and her husband had moved to Haiti, where they built an orphanage and invested their lives in relieving the suffering of widows, street children and orphans.

I picked up the phone. "Hello, Nicole!"

She started right in. "You know that man you played for at the hospital today? That's my dad."

I am fortunate to play music for lots of people, many of whom I will only interact with a handful of times. A step beyond that is being able to have an impact on the life of a person I know and care about.

Rarer still is the opportunity to bless the family of a friend whose life has had a consistent others-oriented focus.

She told me what a wonderfully loving father her dad had been. "He was always caring and providing for the family. Now this disease is wreaking havoc with his brain. The music today was a kiss from Jesus!"

When the phone call ended Connie and I sat in silence, looking at one another through tear-filled eyes, marveling at the unexpected ways God weaves the tapestry of life.

"Everlasting Love"

– CARL CARLTON

I was playing in the hallway when a woman and her grown son walked by carrying bags of food from the cafeteria. The son gave me the once-over and immediately invited me into the room to play for his dad.

In the bed was a man in his mid-seventies. His hands were resting on his chest. His trim, salt-and-pepper mustache gave the impression of a British television detective. On his head was a blue baseball cap with the word "Captain" boldly embroidered in large gold letters and surrounded by decorative golden oak leaves, "scrambled eggs" in Navy lingo. The hat was tilted low, shading his closed eyes.

Our entrance didn't disturb his sleep. The mother and son began discussing what Dad might like to hear, and they settled on anything by Frank Sinatra. "Fly Me to the Moon" is always a good entry point.

As I began to play, Dad's eyes opened slowly as he looked for the source of the sound. He gave a faint smile and then mumbled, "Good, good song."

When I finished, Mom asked, "Did you like that?"

More mumbling. "Nice music. Good, good."

Mom and son continued their conversation while Dad, in his own world, hummed and mumbled. They obviously loved and respected him, but he wasn't an active part of the conversation. It didn't take long to figure out that Dad was dealing with some form of dementia/Alzheimer's in addition to the medical condition that had brought him to this floor.

We continued with another Sinatra classic, "The Way You Look Tonight." Now Dad was getting livelier, keeping time by tapping his fingers on his stomach. Unlike folks with memory issues who exhibit aggression due to their mental confusion, this fellow was different. He had a gentle demeanor, happy, even jovial.

"You know," his wife said, "he was really a big Elvis fan when he was young. In our early days together, he was a drummer."

"You ain't nothing but a hound dog, cryin' all the time."

"Yes, hound dog." He laughed. Now he was smiling and playing his stomach like a snare drum. After a few more Elvis tunes, he was ready to rest.

I dropped in again two days later. It was just the "Captain" and his wife this time. We visited for a few minutes, then repeated some of the songs from before. He was again engaged, but his drumming was interspersed with brief moments of nodding off to sleep.

While he was resting, his wife told me how much the whole family enjoyed music. Most of their grandchildren were taking band

and guitar lessons. She had worked for an accounting firm that did tax preparation for several well-known local musicians. She and her husband had been backstage guests at many concerts and enjoyed their connection with the central Ohio music community.

I mentioned that it seemed like they were dealing with more than the Captain's physical health.

"Yes," she said. "Over fifty years, he's always been such a wonderful husband, father, and friend. We always talked through all our decisions. Sadly, we can't do that now. It's very lonely."

When he roused, she told me, "His favorite song of all time is 'Dancing Queen' by ABBA. I would be surprised if you know that, though."

Well, I thought, *I would be surprised if I knew that too.* But thanks to a student from years before, "Dancing Queen" was tucked away in a folder on my tablet.

Following the performance principle of "Save the best for last," I warmed up my ABBA chops with "Take a Chance on Me." That definitely got the Captain's attention. When I launched into "Dancing Queen," his percussion talents rose to new heights. His chest, stomach, and the bed railings were all now part of the drum kit. His wife was thrilled. "That's great, honey. You're playing the drums!"

On my third visit the following week, we ran through all the favorites. Sinatra music was the starting point, and an exuberant "Dancing Queen" was the finale. During one of the nod-offs, I asked about the Captain's hat.

"He was in the Navy and he was a captain, but that hat's a souvenir. He was never on a ship. We lived in Virginia for many years, and he worked in a top-secret location, overseeing nuclear submarine war games."

From the first time I met this couple and their son, I sensed a strong bond of affection, a deep and abiding care for one another. I've played for hundreds of weddings, all of which include some form of "for better, for worse, for richer, for poorer, in sickness and health, until death do us part." Here was a real-life example of that commitment. A man who had been entrusted with the secrets and strategies of our nation's military defense system was now being equally loved and praised for his ability to tap out the rhythm of a catchy pop tune.

Unconditional love—being loved for who we are, not because of what we can do.

14

Coda

"The Times They Are A-Changin'"

– BOB DYLAN

The cancer floor where I've spent most of my time has thirty-two rooms, each of which is filled with layer upon layer of memories.

If I stepped into room 7214, would I find the crew of construction workers sitting uneasily in their Carhartts and hoodies, trying to comfort their buddy and his wife? He, too tired to speak, and she, too sad to respond. The work buddies are saying anything that will push back the unbearable silence. They are trying to communicate, "We love you, man" without having to add, "We're going to miss you."

Dave, the most vocal of the group, tries to carry the burden of the conversation, but there isn't anyone able to help with the lifting. Most attempts begin with "Remember that job..." The guys respond with a nod and a grunt. The conversation drops. These are men who speak with their actions, not their words. Finally, in desperation Dave says, "Joe, remember that job in Akron when we went to that bar and those women offered to show us their titties for $5.00?" Joe smiles, the guys chuckle, but memories of their rough and rowdy days aren't enough to push back the sadness. Maybe some music will help. *"I hear the train a-coming, it's coming round the bend..."*

But in that same room there are other memories. I might find Kathy and her husband. She with her tablet in hand, ready to sing traditional folks songs as I accompany her on guitar. Her husband ready to do anything that will make his soulmate comfortable. This memory goes back to COVID days. I told Kathy that I had been instructed not to sing for fear of spreading the virus. She said, "They told you not to sing, but no one said anything to me about it. You do the guitar part, and I'll take care of the vocals." Onward we go. "How about 'The Work of the Weavers' by the Clancy Brothers?" Aye, lassie, what would we do if it wasn't for the work of the weavers?

If I go to the north end of the hallway and stop in room 7220, I might find the lawyer standing by the bed, looking out the window, vigorously discussing business with a client, seemingly unaware that he's attached to an infusion line. Or maybe today it will be my guitar buddy with his huge smile. No, I remember now, he's in heaven, scheduling pickin' parties.

At the south end of the hall, will I find the lady with snow-white hair who can only mumble? She looks like she may enjoy classical music, but when her kids arrive, they tell me Tom Petty is her favorite artist and "Free Falling" is her favorite song. Maybe I'll find Mark, my other guitar-playing buddy, who didn't tell me he was a professional jazz guitarist when he booked five lessons with me. He just wanted to learn a little something about folky fingerstyle and arrange the opportunity for us to become friends.

Elvis might still be in residence in room 7224. No, he's off to another fund raiser. Maybe I'll see the sweet grandmother whose son is a member of the Israeli Orchestra. Wait, he's already come and gone. We met once when we serenaded his grandmother in this room and a second time when we played together at the memorial service.

Another layer of memory in this room is the kalimba player with his lovely mom or, on a different day, my missionary friend's dad setting off the bed alarm, scrambling to the door to find out who's making that music. Could he hear the sound of the kalimba? I still feel it resonating within these walls.

Directly across the hall in room 7226, I may find the man who told me, "I don't know why they brought me here. I'm in great shape. Let me out of this bed. I'll do twenty pushups right now." The nurse asks him if he knows where he is. He replies, "I don't know why they brought me here. I'm in great shape. Let me out of this bed and I'll do twenty pushups right now." I ask if he would like to hear a song. "I don't know why they brought me here. I'm in great shape. Let me out of this bed..."

Maybe today I'll see Bobby sneaking through the door of this room. He's returning from a quick smoke break. He thinks no one has noticed, but the nurse smells where he has been. She doesn't scold; the harm of one more cigarette won't make the damage done by the previous 50,000 much worse. At least he isn't trying to flush the butts down this room's toilet anymore.

Maybe my friend Mark is still in room 7206. Will I find him encouraging his wife and friends after the doctor has delivered that devastating prognosis? "Hey people, I'm not dead yet! Let's enjoy the time we have together today!" I will soon hear more of his amazing spiritual journey through the words spoken by his eloquent wife and sons at the memorial service. Or maybe my fiddler friend will be in this room today, ready to play music for his church folks but lacking an instrument. Would you like to borrow my guitar?

All of these rooms, filled with so many stories.

As I write this in the fall of 2022, the in-patient cancer care unit where I've spent most of my time is preparing to move to a new floor in a new area of the hospital. The new area has been updated and remodeled to accommodate the latest promising developments in cancer treatment. At this moment, the shiny new rooms are empty and waiting, preparing for the people who will layer on their own stories and memories.

Automobiles replaced the horse and buggy; cell phones are replacing land lines. All indications are that a new era of cancer care is on the horizon. Thanks to the perseverance and diligence of many brilliant doctors and researchers, thanks to the generosity of individuals and institutions, thanks to the participation of patients who have joined clinical studies, this cruel disease is being brought to its knees. Old treatments are being refined. New treatments are on the way.

The new treatments come with acronyms: BMT (bone marrow transplant), CAR-T (chimeric antigen receptor - T cell). The use of genetics and the power of tweaking our own cancer-fighting immune system holds great promise.

All of this is happening at the same time I am approaching retirement (from the hospital, not from music). I have been a witness to 21st-century, state-of-the-art cancer treatment delivered by caring professionals. Medical treatments will continually develop and improve. What won't change is the ability of music to augment and assist the healing process.

It is my hope that the experiences recorded in this book will inspire a new generation of musicians to fully embrace their calling to entertain, teach, and heal. The mission, if you choose to accept it, is to carry this ancient art into the future.

"The Road Not Taken"

– ROBERT FROST

In the prelude to this book, I mentioned the little rowboat that has carried me through this life. It was small, slow, and not desirable in the eyes of most people. Before I launched my career as an artist-in-residence, two more attractive vessels floated my way.

The first was a speedboat that whizzed by and seemed impossible to catch. When I discovered Martha Stewart was using portions of my music as bumper music (the music going in and out of commercials) for her television show, it got my attention. Around the same time, I received a call from a CBS music supervisor requesting permission to use 27 seconds of "Wheels on the Bus" from *Happy Children, Happy Day*. It would be the opening music for an episode of *The Good Wife*. The thought of getting my music placed in TV and movies was enticing, but I wasn't sure that music placement was the best boat for me.

The second and most interesting opportunity arrived in the form of a sleek schooner. An out-of-the-blue email landed unexpectedly. The sender, a fellow named John Huling, was a musician with a long and successful career. He had heard some of my music on Atmospheres, a cable TV music channel. He floated the idea of having a series of phone conversations to talk about music. All of that was very cool, but the words that grabbed my attention were, "I occasionally chop wood with my neighbor, Will Ackerman. He lives on the other side of the mountain."

Will Ackerman is a builder—of buildings, businesses, and careers. In the early 70s, he was a carpenter in southern California and eventually started his own business, Windham Hill Builders. During his college years, he began experimenting with the acoustic guitar. Instead of sticking with standard tuning, he made up tunings and discovered rich, relaxing melodies along the way. In time, friends told him he should make a record, so he did.

The record landed in the right hands and right places, and it wasn't long till Will was building Windham Hill Records, an independent label known for beautiful, genre-defying instrumental music. Three of the label's foundational artists were Will, his cousin Alex DeGrassi, and the inimitable Michael Hedges. Each of these guitarists has his own unique approach to the instrument. They and the other Windham Hill artists who followed were a huge boon to the world of instrumental music and significant influences on my musical development.

John Huling was also a highly successful recording artist with over twenty-five albums to his name. His music is magical and immersive. Featuring Native American flute and natural sounds, it is evocative of the rugged beauty of America's Southwest. His career has spanned more than forty years.

Having the opportunity to hang out or work with either of these guys would be a treat and a privilege.

After a half dozen phone conversations covering topics from musical styles to the photography of Ansel Adams, I was invited for a weekend visit to John's home. He and his wife were wonderful hosts. They arranged for me to stay nearby in a quaint, quiet motel with a stunning view of the Green Mountains.

We spent most of Saturday together, engaged in a pleasant, ongoing musical dialogue. In the afternoon, John took me to his studio for some demo recording. When we finished, he began asking a few questions that I quickly realized were critical to his reason for initially contacting me.

"How do you feel about exploring alternative tunings?"

I didn't feel that I had plumbed the depths of standard tuning, so I responded, "I occasionally use Dropped D, but not much beyond that."

"Have you written anything at a tempo around 60 or 70 beats per minute?"

Most of what I had written was twice that fast. There was a slight change in the atmosphere; a decision had been made. I realized immediately that my answers were honest but wrong. I wouldn't be a fit for whatever John had in mind. Our conversation was still friendly, but it was clear this ship would sail without me.

My consolation prize was a tasty dinner at the local Mexican cantina. John's wife joined us. Our talk was now about the local history of the Green Mountains and the historical role of the soldiers from Vermont during the Revolutionary War.

When we went back to the house, the three of us sat in the living room for a while. At one point, the conversation drifted back to music. In a voice that seemed as though he was addressing himself and me at the same time, John said, "You're going to make it."

We ended the evening with a handshake. The next day was a long nine-and-a-half-hour drive back home.

You're going to make it. That small piece of encouragement was something I kept in my back pocket for many years.

Disappointed? Yes. Looking back, I realize I was fortunate to have received this level of consideration. Even so, it was not the outcome I wanted. The future I had envisioned was one of increased name recognition. Not rock star fame, but at least a reputation that would create channels and resources for new creative projects. A career that would include hanging out with other known musicians and sailing around the world making great music in beautiful venues. That seemed like the ideal musical life. But that didn't happen.

What did happen reminds me of Robert Frost's lovely poem.

"The Road Not Taken"

Two roads diverged in a yellow wood,
And sorry I could not travel both
And be one traveler, long I stood
And looked down one as far as I could
To where it bent in the undergrowth;

Then took the other, as just as fair,
And having perhaps the better claim,
Because it was grassy and wanted wear;
Though as for that the passing there
Had worn them really about the same,

And both that morning equally lay
In leaves no step had trodden black.
Oh, I kept the first for another day!
Yet knowing how way leads on to way,
I doubted if I should ever come back.

I shall be telling this with a sigh
Somewhere ages and ages hence:
Two roads diverged in a wood, and I—
I took the one less traveled by,
And that has made all the difference.

For every road taken, a thousand roads remain untrod.

A short time after my visit with John, my rowboat arrived. It was what I had been waiting for all along without knowing it. It was a call that made sense to me, "and that has made all the difference."

Instead of being a globe-trotting musician, I've had a life of modest but satisfying musical success, surrounded by wonderfully supportive friends and family. The blessing of presenting music to an audience of one, two, or three people at a time has been the most rewarding work of my life. I've had the honor of singing people into heaven and bringing light into dark places.

It is my hope that this brief selection of stories has been an encouragement to you, my friend, to move forward in your calling and giftings; and that in losing your self-styled future, you may find the life that you were meant to live.

"How Sweet It Is (To Be Loved by You)"

- JAMES TAYLOR (1975), MARVIN GAYE (1964)

"Meet me on 6 Blue at 1:30. We've had a request from a patient. She wants her sons to experience what we do." Jen, whose superpower is connecting with patients, is also an expert at weaving together art and music.

The patient is a woman we met six months earlier during her infusion treatment. She and Jen have completed numerous art and jewelry projects. Sadly, this patient is getting near the end and preparing for hospice care. Her sons have traveled across the country to be with their mom. She has invited Jen and me to bring our gifts to her family circle.

We meet at the appointed time and step into the room. The woman in the bed, Mom, isn't old; in fact, she's clearly middle aged and shows no obvious evidence of her declining condition. On the couch by the window is the older of two young men, totally fixated on his phone screen. Ahh, I think, classic avoidance behavior. Mom's imminent departure is so deep and painful, he's retreating into his electronics. In the recliner by the bed is the younger son. He's a handsome lad in his mid-twenties, a beaming presence by his mother's side.

Jen begins the conversation, a friendly rehearsal of art projects she and Mom have collaborated on during the past months. It's a joyful recounting, and there's no mention of the hard conversations and tears that are now in the past.

Today their final project is a polymer clay handprint. Jen opens the bag, kneads and flattens the material. Mom will press her unique palm and fingerprints into the cool, white clay. Over the next few days, she and the boys may choose to add meaningful tokens to this memorial, loving reminders of the hands that held and raised two fine young men.

"How about some music?" Mom asks. "My guys are very musical."

The older son is still quietly focused on his phone; the younger son asks me, "What do you know by James Taylor?"

The first song is simply a musical reflection of what I see going on in front of me, "Shower the People You Love with Love." After that, a request for "Bad, Bad Leroy Brown." The atmosphere lightens. It's not just me smiling and singing. More upbeat pop tunes follow.

During the concert, Jen is making sure the handprint is properly seated in the clay, capturing every arch, loop, column, and ridge. She again encourages the guys to add something meaningful to the slowly hardening clay, then she says goodbye. Her work here is done. This will be their last project. Onward to the next room.

Mom turns to me. "This may be a stretch, but do you know anything by the Who? Maybe 'Won't Get Fooled Again'?" Mom and the boys are well-rounded music lovers, with a slight bias towards 70's rock. In years of sitting by hundreds of bedsides, I've received all kinds of requests, but today is the first for this classic rock, politically charged, stadium-shaking song. I won't be reaching 112 dB, but there will be windmills!

The older son looks up and says, "I got the info, Mom. You're all set."

Looks like I misunderstood his focus on the phone. He wasn't retreating; he was smoothing the path for Mom's transition to hospice care. Now he is fully present.

Mom laughingly asks him, "Why don't you sing something? I want you to put that performance degree to work." Yipes! I'm glad I didn't know he was a graduate of the prestigious Julliard School of Music when I started this concert!

No surprise, he asks for show tunes. We begin with "New York, New York," then on to "The Way You Look Tonight," "Fly Me to the Moon," and more. Then the younger brother brings it back to mellow jazz and pop, Lionel Richie and more James Taylor. Mom says, "He's a triple threat, acting, singing and dancing. He can do it all." This young man has pipes and personality!

I have spent almost an hour in this room on the cancer floor, a room filled with love and laughter. I should be moving down the hall, but still we find time for one... no, two more songs. Everyone here knows that Mom's forever departure is near, but we live in the present, not in the future. Today we will laugh and we will sing. We'll not worry about tomorrow; tomorrow will worry about itself.

In two days, I will be retiring from two decades of playing music for cancer patients.

In two weeks, I will receive a call. "Mom is gone." The younger son and I will share memories of our time together with his family. In some small way, I have been adopted into this loving circle of creative people. Music and art opened a door, created a safe space, and fashioned a joyful moment even in the shadow of death.

Music has again worked its magic. It's always the same... and never the same.

Thanks to

Jennifer Jarrett, for knowing where I was and what I was doing.

Jen McHale, friend, co-laborer, and sounding board.

Kitchen Kapers, for opening the door through funding and support.

Kevin Ryan and Kim McClelland, longtime friends and fellow guitar fanatics.

Elaine Starner, friend and editor, for knowing how to shape a bundle of rambling tales into a coherent story line.

The Smiths (Don and Debbie), The McClellands (Kim and Katherine), and all the friends who encouraged me to "write that down."

Tim Johnson, friend, fellow jammer, and professional photographer

Mom and Dad (Ken and Barbara Morgan), for a lifetime of encouragement and support.

The kids: David, Christen, and Ben, for being who you are and bringing so much joy and encouragement into my life.

Connie, best friend, wife, co-writer, and pre-editor. You have made this journey possible and life wonderful. Thanks for bringing the humanity into this book.

Discography

Original Instrumental Music

The Journey - Places Real and Imagined (1996). This is a solo acoustic guitar instrumental autobiography of my growing up years. It gained some attention from *Echoes*, a nationally syndicated radio program hosted by John Diliberto. The title cut from was included on Volume 3 of a sampler disc released by Acoustic Music Resource. (Solo acoustic guitar Taylor 710c)

Stories (1999). On this project, the acoustic guitar, a Ryan Mission Grand, is joined by bass, percussion, voice, and flute. "John's delicate fingerstyle guitar melodies are quite captivating, taking the listener into a world that is teeming with optimism, joy, and friendly Stories. Highly recommended to all lovers of acoustic guitar music." - *Musical Soundscapes*

Motionography (2006) is about *movement*: flight, swimming, dancing, as well as places: the moon, oceans, and stars. It's the *sound of one guitar*, fingers dancing, sounds splashing, sonic canvas, air art, wooden heart made flesh, steel strings spring to life, moving, across the star field accompanied by dancers, singers, swimmers, writing rhythm, resonating life. (Guitar: Taylor 710c)

Quiet World (2014) is a collection of 16 acoustic guitar-based songs that grew out of my work as an Artist-in-Residence. This project offers a musical perspective of the experiences and emotions observed in people battling cancer. The music - acoustic guitar keyboard, voice, flute, button box, and percussion - conveys a strong sense of hope, optimism, and joy, even in the midst of difficult circumstance. (Guitar: Ryan Nightingale Grand Soloist)

In This Moment (2015). In the middle of recording *Quiet World* - it took over a year to pull all the pieces together - I sat down one afternoon thinking, "I should be able to get a recording project completed in less than a year!" I spent two afternoons recording a dozen spontaneous tunes which were released the following year as *In This Moment*. (Guitar: Ryan Nightingale Grand Soloist)

The Other Side of Silence (2018). When I first submitted *Quiet World* to Pandora, it was rejected. I figured it was because the music didn't fit easily into a specific category, too jazzy to be folky, too folky to be easy listening. I asked my engineer buddy, Tom Boyer, if he could send me a mix of *Quiet World* with guitar only. He did, and when that recording was submitted as *The Other Side of Silence*, it was accepted. Don't ask me what the name means, but I'm hoping it sounds relaxing. Later, when I resubmitted *Quiet World* it was accepted too. Better late than never! (Guitar: Ryan Nightingale Grand Soloist)

Perspective (2021). A friend asked me to write a few solo guitar pieces that might work as backing tracks for movie trailers. He had an inside connection to that market. Failing to realize that movie trailers are almost aways performed by hyper-dramatic synthesizers, I recorded a handful of ad-libbed solo guitar pieces. The movie connection fell through but the tunes stayed on my recorder. When I gave them a listen a few years later, I thought, "Not too shabby." It's just a matter of perspective. (Guitar: Ryan Nightingale Grand Soloist)

12 String Adventures (2022). My buddy Jim Doyle brough his beautiful 12-string Guild to the house one day. It had just been set-up, cleaned-up, and was wearing shiny new strings. He said, "Keep this for a few days and check it out." Fresh musical ideas were popping off the strings; ahh, the lovely 12-string shimmer. Fortunately, my digital recorder was close at hand. All the songs were recorded in two afternoons, ad-libbed, one take, no edits. There are some "bumps and burps" in the recording... or did I purposely record it that way? You can be the judge. I loved the jangly sound and the energy. (Guitar: Guild 1989 JF65 – 12)

Christmas Music

Capture the Night (2004) is a collection of Christmas classics arranged for solo acoustic guitar. "Tinsel," the only original tune on the disc, was included on NPR's *All Songs Considered* during Christmas week two years in a row. (Guitar: Taylor 710c)

Music for December (2008). A newly formed local record label asked me to re-record the arrangements from *Capture the Night* in their official studio. We also added two more Christmas classics. (Guitar: Taylor 710c)

Children's Music

Happy Children, Happy Day (2011), Noelle and John. This was a fun little off-the-cuff project with Noelle Shearer, a kind of greatest hits of traditional music for children. "I Love the Flowers," "Itsy Bitsy Spider," etc. The angelic vocals by Noelle Shearer and a lively dialog between the two of us has garnered a lot of attention on numerous music sites. Our arrangement of "Wheels on the Bus" was featured in an episode of "The Good Wife." "Twinkle, Twinkle Little Star" was added to the playlist at the Cottage/Museum of the sisters who wrote this delightful tune—maybe because Noelle sang all the verses.

Dance With the Moon (2020). When it looked like the COVID pandemic might last longer than a few weeks and gigs were beginning to disappear, I used the time to record this grouping of traditional lullabies. The pandemic has come and gone, but even in healthy times these beautiful melodies can bring peace and comfort.

Joy is Everywhere (2023), Noelle and John. When I was cleaning old tracks off my digital recorder, I found several songs that we recorded around the same time as *Happy Children, Happy Day*. Thankfully, most children's music is timeless so they are as fun as ever, even thirteen years later.

Websites of Interest

In case you are interested in learning more about some of the people and topics in this book:

https://www.kitchenkapers.org/ **Kitchen Kapers** raises money for the Ohio Health foundation.

https://eyeswideopenint.org/ **Eyes Wide Open International** is a non-profit that activates, mobilizes, and encourages people to join us in working alongside local and global partners in providing relief to those in the midst of crisis and human suffering. Our specific thrust will be towards those in the greatest need – widows and orphans.

https://www.morganguitar.com/ The adventures of a roving musician.

https://ryanguitars.com/ **Kevin Ryan**, luthier, friend, former bandmate and builder of the finest guitars in the world.

https://www.treeoflifeartworks.com/ **Kim McClelland**, generous friend, fellow musician and amazing scrimshaw artist.

https://tommyemmanuel.com/ **Tommy Emmanuel**, CGP (certified guitar player) born and raised in Australia, the "Wonder from Down Under," a force of nature, master guitarist.

https://williamackerman.com/ **William Ackerman**, guitarist, producer, and founder of Windham Hill Records.

https://johnhuling.com/ **John Huling**, musician, native American flute and natural sounds, one of the most sought after and emulated styles in Native American Music.

https://cityofgallipolis.com/ **Gallipolis**, a beautiful small town on the banks of the Ohio River.